THE RELIGIOUS FAITH
OF GREAT MEN

THE RELIGIOUS FAITH
OF GREAT MEN

By
ARCHER WALLACE

Essay Index Reprint Series

BOOKS FOR LIBRARIES PRESS, INC.
FREEPORT, NEW YORK

First Published 1934
Reprinted 1967

LIBRARY OF CONGRESS CATALOG CARD NUMBER:

67-26792

PRINTED IN THE UNITED STATES OF AMERICA

AUTHOR'S PREFACE

THIS book is an attempt to record, rather than to interpret, the religious thinking of great men. Actual quotations have been given and very little comment has been included.

Representatives have been chosen from various fields and readers will see that there is a wide variety of views, even among men who are in substantial agreement on basic beliefs. For instance, there is wide divergence between the confident affirmations of a statesman like William Ewart Gladstone and the hesitant faith of the statesman Benjamin Franklin, who occasionally was quite sceptical; likewise the faith of Sir Walter Scott or W. M. Thackeray was much more definite than that of Nathaniel Hawthorne or Robert Louis Stevenson. I do not want to make out-and-out believers of men who were undecided about their faith and sometimes quite agnostic. This book is simply an attempt to record the views of many who, in varying degrees, believed in God and accepted the implications of such a belief.

In a book on Napoleon, W. H. Hudson points out that his attitude to religion was uncertain because he talked in different ways at different times to different people: "The opinions which he gave out for consumption were often hopelessly at variance with those which he expressed in confidential intercourse." Undoubtedly this is true of many people and certainly of several dealt with in this book.

I am deeply indebted to my friend and colleague, Rev. George A. Little, D.D., who has carefully read the manuscript and made many excellent suggestions.

ARCHER WALLACE.

Toronto

ACKNOWLEDGMENTS

The author has made every possible attempt to acknowledge the quotations used in this book, first, by a reference to the book at the bottom of the page whereon the quotation is made and, secondly, by giving here a list of the publishers to whose courtesy he is deeply indebted. If there has been any oversight or failure to adequately acknowledge quotations the author offers his apologies and hopes to be forgiven. The following is the list of books quoted together with the authors' and publishers' names:

The Abingdon Press: *Abraham Lincoln the Christian* by William J. Johnstone; *Roosevelt's Religion* by Christian F. Reisner.

E. C. Allen & Co.: *Life of George Peabody* by Hanaford.

George Allen and Unwin Ltd.: *Science and the Unseen World* by Arthur Stanley Eddington; *Viscount Leverhulme* by his son.

Bell and Cockburn: *R. L. S.* by Francis Watt.

Ernest Benn Limited: *John and Sebastian Cabot* by C. Raymond Beazley.

A. L. Burt Company: *History of the English People* by J. R. Green.

Cassell & Co. Ltd.: *The Revolt of Democracy* by Alfred Russell Wallace.

James Clarke and Company: *Sir Walter Scott* by John A. Patten; *Eucken and Bergson, Their Significance for Christian Thought* by E. Hermann; *Christ in Shakespeare* by George H. Morrison.

Constable and Company Ltd.: *Victor Hugo* by Madame Duclaux; *Life of John Bright* by George M. Trevelyan; *Life of Pasteur* by René Vallery-Radot.

Thomas Y. Crowell Company: *Has Science Discovered God?* edited by Edward H. Cotton.

J. M. Dent & Sons, Ltd.: *Life of Bach* by C. F. A. Williams; *Life of Mozart* by Holmes.

Doubleday, Doran and Company, Inc.: *Recollections and Letters of General Lee* by his son.

Duffield and Green: *Tolstoy* by G. R. Noyes.

E. P. Dutton & Co., Inc.: *My Arnold Bennett* by Marguerite, his wife; *Life of Bach* by C. F. A. Williams; *Life of Mozart* by Holmes.

The Epworth Press: *A Faggot of Torches, A Handful of Stars, A Casket of Cameos* and *A Bunch of Everlastings* by F. W. Boreham; *Brothers in Art* by H. W. Shrewsbury; *Christianity and Culture* by John C. Bowran; *Hours with the Immortals* by Robert P. Downes.

The Friendship Press: *Pioneers of Goodwill* by Harold B. Hunting.

The Frontier Press Company: *Masters of Achievement* by Henry W. Ruoff.

Great Thoughts Magazine.

Harper & Brothers: *The Romantic Rise of a Great American* by Russell H. Conwell; *Messages from Master Minds* by J. W. G. Ward; *Spiritual Voices in Modern Literature* by Trevor H. Davies; *The Spiritual Drama in the Life of Thackeray* by Nathaniel Wright Stephenson.

George H. Harrop & Co.: *The Man Napoleon* by W. H. Hudson.

Hodder and Stoughton: *Life of Sir William Hartley* by A. S. Peake; *Life of Sir George Williams* by J. E. Hodder Williams; *Old Memories* by Sir Henry Jones; *Private Prayer in Christian Story* by Jane T. Stoddart.

Henry Holt and Company: *Franz Liszt* by Guy de Pourtalès.

Hutchinson & Co.: *My Religion.*

Kilmarnock Standard: *Life of Robert Burns* by J. C. Higgins.

John Lane and Bodley Head: *Sir Francis Drake* by E. F. Benson; *Sir Walter Raleigh* by Milton Waldman.

Little, Brown & Company: *Cromwell* by G. R. S. Taylor; *Bismarck* by Emil Ludwig; *Franklin, the Apostle of Modern Times* by Bernard Fay; *Woodrow Wilson, an Interpretation* by A. Maurice Low.

Horace Liveright, Inc.: *Napoleon* by Emil Ludwig; *Meet General Grant* by W. E. Woodward.

Lothrop, Lee & Shepard Co.: *How They Succeeded* by O. S. Marden.

The Macmillan Company of Canada Limited: *The Mysterious Universe* by Sir James Jeans; *The Nature of the Physical World* by Arthur Stanley Eddington.

Methodist Book Concern: *Lincoln's Use of the Bible* by S. Trevena Jackson.

Methuen & Co. Ltd.: *Rembrandt* by Elizabeth A. Sharp; *Tennyson* by A. C. Benson; *Reason and Belief* by Sir Oliver Lodge.

Houghton Mifflin Co.: *Nathaniel Hawthorne and His Wife* by Julian Hawthorne; *Quaker Militant, John Greenleaf Whittier* by Albert Mordell; *Harriet Beecher Stowe* by Charles E. Stowe.

John Murray Co.: *The Great Duke* by W. H. Fitchett.

Oliphant, Anderson & Ferrier: *Pilgrims in the Region of Faith* by J. A. Hutton.

Oxford University Press: *Counsels and Ideals* by Sir William Osler.

G. P. Putnam's Sons: *Life of Goethe* by Albert Bielschowsky; *Life of Bismarck* by James W. Headlam.

Fleming H. Revell Co.: *The Battle of Principles* by Newell Dwight Hillis.

Sampson Low, Marston & Co. Ltd.: *Barrie, the Story of a Genius* by J. A. Hammerton.

Charles Scribner's Sons: *The New Reformation* by Michael Pupin; *From Immigrant to Inventor* by Michael Pupin; *Margaret Ogilvy* by her son, J. M. Barrie.

Walter Scott: *Life of Heine* by William Sharp.

Frederick A. Stokes Company: *The Amazing Benjamin Franklin* by H. J. Smythe.

Williams and Norgate: *Present Day Ethics* by Rudolf Eucken.

The John C. Winston Co.: *Thomas A. Edison, Benefactor of Mankind* by Francis Trevelyan Miller.

Yale University Press: *The Evolution of Science and Religion* by Robert A. Millikan.

CONTENTS

CHAPTER ONE

Religious Faith of Great Adventurers

EARLY explorers of the Middle Ages, who sailed across uncharted seas, with very vague ideas as to what lay beyond the horizon, were, in most cases, men of deep religious feeling. Religious faith has much in common with the spirit of adventure. Christopher Columbus was still a very young man when he became possessed with the grand idea which ever after controlled his life. He felt himself to be as much called to open up the New World as other men were to preach the gospel. He said repeatedly that he was a humble but specially selected instrument in God's hands to extend the horizon of man's knowledge. His biographer says that he rejoiced in the name Christopher, for he believed he was chosen to "bear Christ" (which is what the Latin word literally means) across the ocean. Of his deep religious faith, Washington Irving writes:

"Religion mingled with the whole course of his thoughts and actions and shone forth in his most private and unstudied writings. Whenever he made any great discovery he immediately celebrated it by solemn thanks to God. The voice of prayer and the melody of praise rose from his ships when they first beheld the New World, and his first action in landing was to prostrate himself upon the earth and return

3

thanksgiving to Almighty God. Every evening the *Salve Regina* and other hymns were chanted by his crew, and masses were performed in the beautiful groves bordering the wild shores of this heathen land. All his great enterprises were undertaken in the name of the Holy Trinity, and he partook of Communion previous to embarkation. Religion was deep-seated in his soul and diffused a dignity and composure over his whole demeanor. His language was pure and guarded, free from oaths and irreverent expressions."

The Cabots, John and Sebastian, are almost as widely known as Columbus. They were rough, hardy men, these brave adventurers of those far-off days; they were, withal, men of prayer and faith. While crude superstition characterized much of their self-imposed missionary efforts, there is no doubt that the Cabots—and many other explorers of that day—did feel it to be their duty to extend Christianity. With brutal frankness they reported their missionary methods which were often anything but "gently persuasive." Nevertheless they did rejoice that natives who had been idolaters, fond of eating human flesh and fierce and cruel, accepted the Christian faith and became obedient to the Mother Church.

In 1553, new enterprises were under consideration but Sebastian Cabot—then seventy-eight years of age—was too old to take an active part in them. He did, however, draw up a list of thirty-three articles for the instruction of the fleet. This document, the only writings which have come down to us from the Cabots, is full of shrewdness and experienced wisdom. Furthermore, it reveals a depth of religious devotion hardly looked for in the adventurers of such an age. The document urges loyalty and obedience to those in command; warns against the perils of jealousy and dissension and pleads for orderliness. Two of the articles deal entirely with the necessity of religious observances while another frowns upon religious controversy. Articles twelve and thirteen read:

"Item, that no blaspheming of God, or detestable swearing be used in any ship, nor communication of ribaldry, filthy tales, or ungodly talk to be suffered in the company of any ship, neither dicing, carding, tabling, nor other devilish games to be frequented, whereby ensueth not only poverty to the players, but also strife, variance, brawling, fighting, and oftentimes murder, to the . . . destruction of the parties and provoking of God's . . . just wrath. . . . These and all such-like pestilences and contagions of vices and sins to be eschewed, and the offenders once monished, and not reforming, to be punished at the discretion of the Captain and master. . . .

"Item, that morning and evening prayer, with other common services appointed by the King's Majesty and laws of this Realm to be . . . read in every ship daily by the minister in the Admiral and (by) the Merchant, or some other person learned in other ships, and the Bible or Paraphrases to be read devoutly and Christianly to God's honour, and for His Grace to be obtained by humble prayer of the Navigants accordingly." [1]

---

[1] C. Raymond Beazley, *John and Sebastian Cabot*, p. 189.

Among those who were moved by the spirit of adventure to penetrate into vast and little-known regions, a foremost place must be given to William Penn. "When, as a lad of sixteen, William Penn went up to the University, he found to his surprise that Oxford was the home of Thomas Loe. There the good man had already suffered imprisonment for conscience sake. The personality of the Quaker appealed to the reflective temperament of the young student, whilst the good man's sufferings for his convictions awoke his profoundest sympathies. To the horror of his father, he ardently espoused the persecuted cause, involving himself in such disfavor with the authorities of the University that they peremptorily ordered his dismissal.

"Soon after his expulsion from Oxford, he was appointed Victualler of the Squadron lying off Kinsale, and was authorized to reside at, and manage, his father's Irish estate. It was whilst he was thus engaged that Thomas Loe revisited Cork. Penn, of course, attended the meetings. 'It was in this way,' he tells us, 'that God, in His everlasting kindness, guided my feet in the flower of my youth, when about two and twenty years of age. He visited me with a certain testimony of His eternal Word through a Quaker named Thomas Loe.' The text at that memorable and historic service, like a nail in a sure place, fastened itself upon the mind of the young officer.

"Penn was electrified. His whole being was stirred to its depths. 'The undying fires of enthusiasm at once blazed up within him,' one record declares. 'He was exceedingly reached and wept much,' the Quaker chronicle assures us.

He renounced every hope that he had ever cherished in order that he might realize this one. This was in 1666—the year in which London was devoured by the flames.

" 'Penn's conversion,' says Dr. Stoughton, 'was now completed. That conversion must not be regarded simply as a change of opinion. It penetrated his moral nature. It made him a new man. He rose into another sphere of spiritual life and consciousness.' " [2] In 1681, Penn inherited from his father a debt against the English government of sixteen thousand pounds. He agreed to accept, as satisfaction for this, an extensive belt of land lying west of the Delaware River and north of Maryland. Penn sailed from England on October 27, 1682.

Within a generation a great host of people began to move westward from Europe, but when Penn arrived the white settlements were sparsely populated and many dangers menaced the newcomers, chief among them being the deep-seated hatred of the Indians. Immediately after his arrival Penn did an extraordinary thing. He called together the Indians and met them under an elm tree that is now marked by a monument. To their amazement he came unarmed and they in turn threw away their bows and arrows. Then very solemnly Penn made a treaty with the savage men of the forest. He told them that he wanted nothing but their friendship. He called God to witness his promise that neither he, nor any of his friends, would injure the Indians in any way. They in turn bound themselves to do the same.

---

[2] F. W. Boreham, *A Handful of Stars*, pp. 12, 13.

The historian, Bancroft, says: "This treaty of peace was made under the open sky, by the side of the Delaware, with the sun, and the river, and the forest for witnesses. It was not confirmed by formal oaths, nor ratified by signatures and seals; no written record of the conference can be found, and its terms and conditions had no abiding monument, but on the heart. The simple sons of the wilderness, returning to their wigwams, kept the history of the covenant by strings of wampum, and, long afterwards in their cabins, they would count over the shells on a clean piece of bark and recall to their own memory, and repeat to their children, or to the stranger, the words of William Penn."

William Penn had deep religious convictions, and one of these was that it was possible to win men by love. He read and re-read the Sermon on the Mount, and especially those passages which have to do with the treatment of one's enemies. He resolved to conquer the savage Indians but to do it by showing the spirit of Jesus Christ, and he succeeded magnificently. Bancroft writes: "His name was fondly cherished as a household word in the cottages of the old world; and not a tenant of a wigwam from the Susquehannah to the sea doubted his integrity. His fame is as wide as the world; he is one of the few who have gained abiding glory."

Of Sir Francis Drake, most colorful of all the picturesque men of Elizabeth's day, old Thomas Fuller wrote: "This our captain was a religious man towards God and His houses, generally sparing churches, where he came; chaste in his life; just in his dealings; true to his word; and merciful to those who were under him; hating nothing so much as idleness."

Not less significant is the earnest request of Francis Drake, for the prayers of John Fox, author of *The Book of Martyrs*. After his triumph at Cadiz in 1587, Drake wrote: "To the right reverend godly learned father; my very good friend, Mr. Fox, preacher of the Word of God. Master Fox, whereas we have had of late such happy success against the Spaniards, I do assure myself you have faithfully remembered us in your good prayers, and therefore I have not forgotten briefly to make you a partaker thereof."

In commenting on this striking letter, a biographer of Drake writes: "The veteran divine was dead as the words were penned, but such prayers we may well believe were breathed with his latest sighs. In the letter, Drake gives Fox a short account of the operations, and ends with a renewed request for his prayers, 'That we may have continued praise in Israel,' and signs himself 'Your loving friend and faithful son in Jesus Christ.' Then comes this postscript, 'Our enemies are many but our Protector commandeth the whole world. Let us all pray continually and our Lord Jesus will hear us in good time mercifully.' "[3]

"All the time, in that age in which religion was a real force, a cause for which men went singing to stake or block, there lay behind his swearings and severities, his fun and his foul temper, a deep and ferocious faith that God was with him, and that it was under His direct and special protection

---

[3] *Drake and the Tudor Nancy*, Vol. II, p. 105.

that he flew his flag, and for His glory that he pounded the Spaniard. Every despatch that Drake ever wrote reporting his achievements and outlining his future aims (when he condescended to communicate them) was based on that absolute conviction. 'The grace of God' in his mouth was no conventional form of words: it was the sober defined expression of his trust in the power of the Almighty. Perhaps today we should call such a man a religious fanatic, or, if we consider his career of frank piracy, a hypocrite, but either verdict would be the very reverse of the truth. He prayed to God, fervently and constantly, not from fanatic mania, but because he was the simplest and most consistent of Christians, and he singed the King of Spain's beard in the name of Jesus Christ, because the King of Spain was a damnable swindler and a torturer of Protestants, and an enemy of England." [4]

Sir Walter Raleigh, whose moral character was somewhat of an enigma, was one of the striking figures of Queen Elizabeth's day. He was versatile in his interests and at times seemed to be actuated by the highest motives; on other occasions he was cruel, sordid and brutal. That he was a fearless soldier with a passionate love of adventure is certain. He served thirteen months in Ireland when Lord Grey was Deputy for the Queen. The natives of that unhappy land were in constant rebellion and a biographer of Raleigh writes: "During his thirteen months in Ireland his sword was never idle for the insurrection smouldered on."

During subsequent years his love of adventure found ample

---

[4] E. F. Benson, *Sir Francis Drake*, pp. 227-228.

opportunity. Inordinate ambition made him countless enemies. "His one fault," wrote John Aubrey in his *Lives of Eminent Men*, "was that he was damnably proud." He gained and lost public favor many times; his hatred towards Spain made him a popular hero but eventually cost him his life for he was executed at the insistence of Spain. When he knew death was inevitable he died with serenity and dignity.

Raleigh's religious sense seems to have been much the same as that of many eminent men of his day. Because of that these words of his biographer have significance: "Despite the frequent references to and preoccupation with religion to be seen in his verse and even more strongly in his prose, it cannot be urged that Raleigh was in any profound sense a religious person. His Puritanism, as I trust I have made clear, was a habit of thought rather than an ecstatic union with the Deity under the peculiar forms of Puritanism —and that habit of thought merely led him, if not to constant practice, at least to an Old Testament view of right conduct as a necessity lest one be punished. . . . His weaknesses appear in his discourses on conduct, as we should expect. Expediency guided his own life all too largely, and it is the corner-stone of his moral philosophy. All his life he pondered on the soul and its immortality, like a good Puritan, yet his mature conclusions on the subject are worthy of the grossest materialist:

"'For we worship God because our souls are made to his image, and we know that he is *a rewarder of them that serve him* . . . now to what end were religion, if there were no reward? and what reward is there if the souls do not live forever?'

"And in his advice to his beloved son, wherein the wise and experienced father sets forth for the young man's benefit all that he has learned from life, he counsels him never to trust any man too much, to marry for convenience rather than for love, to please God lest he be punished. There is no suggestion of purity of heart or integrity of character, of the beauty of passionately losing one's self in love for a friend or a woman or one's Creator. He did not see the humour of warning his son to be careful in marriage, he who went to prison for his espousal of the lad's mother, nor of the man at whose jewels and raiment all the world marvelled saying:

" 'Exceed not in the humour of rags and bravery, for these will soon wear out the fashion; but money in thy purse will ever be in fashion; and no man is esteemed for gay garments but by fools and women.' Luckily, though he preached like Polonius, he could act like Lærtes, and it was the practice rather than the precept to which the son for whom this was written paid regard." [5]

Sir John Franklin was another fearless adventurer whose fame is enduring. In 1820, when he was thirty-four years of age, he was in charge of an expedition into the far north. He was compelled to spend a winter at Fort Enterprise, a lonely and ice-bound place between Great Bear Lake and

---

[5] Milton Waldman, *Sir Walter Raleigh*, pp. 90 and 187.

Great Slave Lake. In the long period of waiting he found in reading the Bible a source of delight and profit. He discovered in it new beauty and marvelled that he had so little appreciated its truth and beauty.

In a letter written to his sister at that time, he said: "If, under conviction of sin, a man should enquire, 'How can I be saved,' would it not be joy unspeakable for him to find out that the Gospel points the way. Christ, who died for the salvation of sinners, is the Way, the Truth and the Life. Whoso cometh unto him in full purpose of heart shall in no wise be cast out. Can anything be more cheering than these assurances, or better calculated to fill the mind with heavenly impressions and lift up the heart in grateful adoration to God?"

He sailed from England in an effort to discover the Northwest Passage on May 19, 1845. When after months of weary waiting he did not return, expeditions were sent out in search of him, and the relics and skeletons found on the coast of an inhospitable island, proved that he and his men had perished of starvation and exposure in 1847.

From the time of his conversion in 1820 until, when twenty-seven years later, Sir John Franklin died on the bleak coast of a northern isle, he was cheered and inspired by a sense of the divine presence which supported him on whatever seas he sailed. A midshipman on Franklin's ship wrote home an enthusiastic letter about his captain: "He is quite a bishop," wrote this youth, "we have church morning and evening on Sundays, the evening service is held in the cabin to allow of the attendance of the watch that could not be present in the forenoon. We go both times. The men say they would rather have him than half the parsons of England."

The tragic death of Sir Ernest Shackelton is still a fresh memory. After his first attempt to reach the South Pole he returned to England and described, as far as it was possible to describe in words, the agony of a long, weary journey over the glaciers and icy wastes of southern Georgia. It has been referred to as one of the most magnificent feats of courage and endurance ever known. In his book, *South,* he has left a thrilling account of that feat of indomitable perseverance. He writes: "When I look back upon those days, with all their anxiety and peril, I cannot doubt that our party was divinely guided, both over the snowfields and across the stormswept sea. I know that, during the long and racking march of thirty-six hours over the unnamed mountains and glaciers of southern Georgia, it seemed to me, very often, that we were not three but four. I said nothing to my companions on the point, but afterwards, Worsley said to me: 'Boss, I had a curious feeling on the march that there was Another Person with us.' "

Just before he left England for the last time, Sir Ernest again spoke of his deep sense of God's presence on his journeys. To the writer, Harold Begbie, he quoted the 139th Psalm: "If I take the wings of the morning, and dwell in the uttermost parts of the sea, even there shall thy hand lead me and thy right hand shall hold me." "That Psalm," said he, "exactly fitted our case."

"To another sea," wrote his friend Begbie, "he has now sailed his ship, a sea of silence, darkness and mystery, but with a coastline glowing in the rays of a brighter sun. Across that sea many greater spirits have sailed, but few, I think, with steadier hearts and eyes more eager for new shores."

The list of adventurous men who went out like Abraham, not knowing the goal, but with unshaken trust in God, is a long one. Whether they pushed forward into the tropical jungle, or trudged across bleak Arctic wastes, they believed with Browning:

> "I see my way as birds their trackless way,
> I shall arrive! What time, what circuit first,
> I ask not, but unless God sends His hail,
> Or blinding fire balls, or sleet, or shifting snow,
> In some good time—His good time—I shall arrive;
> He guides me and the bird. In His good time."

CHAPTER TWO

Religious Faith of Great Artists

MICHELANGELO has been accused of deliberately living in sadness. Probably this was correct. He was often unhappy. Two thousand years after the Hebrew prophet Jeremiah uttered his bitter protest against the world in which he lived, Michelangelo designed a fresco of him. He began the work in 1508, when he was thirty-four years of age, and finished it four years later. In the gloomy, austere figure of Jeremiah the great artist typified himself. But depression generally indicates sincerity, and of the religious conviction and sincerity of Michelangelo there can be no question. He was capable of moods of almost inconsolable despair.

In 1533, just thirteen years after the death of Raphael, Michelangelo began his most famous fresco, "The Last Judgement," on the altar wall of the Sistine Chapel. It was a stupendous task to which the painter devoted eight of the best years of his life. The composition is forty-seven feet long by forty-three feet wide, was completed in 1541 and as far as painting is concerned marked the peak of the artist's work.

He was intensely religious, although his independent and haughty disposition brought him into sharp conflict with ecclesiastical authorities on several occasions. He forced imperial popes to regard him as an equal and braved their displeasure, an historian says, "more than a king would have done." Ordinary pleasures he viewed with contempt and although he might have lived in luxury he was generally content with a crust of bread. Most of his possessions including statues and pictures he gave to friends and relatives.

He found inspiration in good books and particularly in the solemn grandeur of the Bible. The Hebrew prophets never failed to awaken in him the purest and deepest emotions. One of the sorrows of his life—and he had many—was to see his friend, Savonarola, bound to the pillory, strangled and burned; whose "living word," he wrote, "will always remain branded in my soul."

Practically all he did, either with stone or on canvas, centred around religious themes. When he was asked to paint the ceiling of the Sistine Chapel at Rome he protested to Pope Julius II that he was not a painter but a sculptor, yet after he had devoted himself absolutely to this work for four years, and the scaffolding was removed, a result had been achieved which is without parallel.

On the ten thousand square feet of ceiling there are three hundred and thirty-three principal figures of colossal size besides a vast number of others. He prepared himself for the task by months of close scrutiny of the Bible text, by studying the poetry of Dante, and almost breaking his heart over the sermons of Savonarola. Michelangelo himself preached with his brush and chisel with as passionate intensity as ever evangelist did. He died at Rome on February

18, 1564, after dictating his brief will: "I commit my soul to God, my body to the earth, and my property to my nearest relatives."

When Leonardo da Vinci passed along the streets of Milan or Florence the admiring people whispered: "There he goes to paint the 'Last Supper.'" Although much of the original glory of this great picture has faded it is still the most famous painting in the world. Leonardo began his greatest work, "The Last Supper," in the refectory of a Dominican convent in 1496 and it was completed in two years. It was painted on the wall in oil and to this circumstance many attribute its premature decay. Fortunately many copies of the painting were made and the one by Marco Oggioni, now in London, has been done with remarkable skill. "Leonardo's 'Last Supper,'" one critic writes, "although now a mere ruin, was probably the greatest composition ever produced, and it was undoubtedly the earliest."

A critic writes of Leonardo: "He cast a spell over his own age, and other ages as well. And to what can we ascribe this wonderful spell, this charm and influence, if not to the pure spiritual fire which burned within him, and which, all his life through, drove him hither and thither in search of truth and beauty, and which may be said to bear some likeness to the spirit of Christ Himself? . . . Beneath all his moods of fitfulness there lay a placid strength and deep-set joy in the service of Jesus whom he called the Prime mover."

He was amazingly versatile in his gifts. "He excelled in

many physical exercises, was an accomplished musician, and possessed, besides, a captivating eloquence. He was intensely ambitious, haughty, capricious, dreamy, and restless; and undoubtedly it may be laid to his gigantic conceptions, unattainable ideals of perfection, and his insatiable thirst after new achievements, that he left only three or four works of supreme beauty and perfection. Not only every art, but almost every science studied in his time seems to have engaged his attention. He was familiar with chemistry, geometry, anatomy, botany, mechanics, and optics; and there is scarcely a subject that he touched in which he did not, in more or less important points, anticipate the discoveries of later philosophers and scientists. His *Treatise on Painting* has been translated into many languages, and is the foundation of all that has been written on the art." [1]

His character was strongly religious and singularly beautiful. He was fond of animals and would not eat them. He bought caged birds in the market and set them free. He lived frugally but protested that he was not poor, "I am not poor," he said, "only he is poor whose wants are many." He frequently associated with the aristocracy of his day but he remained uncorrupted. In his diary he wrote, what was certainly true in his case, "Intellectual passion drives away all lusts."

Not less than Michelangelo was Leonardo an evangelist in art. He toiled with indomitable perseverance and restless energy to make real those scenes of Holy Writ which had so completely captured his whole being. When painting

---

[1] *Masters of Achievement*, pp. 126, 127.

"The Last Supper," he left the head of Jesus unfinished because he did not venture to portray the heavenly dignity which ought to distinguish the Master. Often when he attempted to paint Jesus his agitation and emotion were intense. Among his most celebrated paintings and frescos are: "St. John the Baptist"; "The Madonna Seated on the Lap of St. Anne"; "The Annunciation"; "The Virgin of the Rocks" and "The Last Supper."

In 1550, just thirty-one years after Da Vinci's death, Giorgio Vasari wrote *Lives of the Most Eminent Painters,* in which he tells of the artist's death in the following words: "Finally, having become old, he lay sick for many months, and, finding himself near death, wrought diligently to make himself acquainted with the Catholic ritual, and with the good and holy path of the Christian religion: he then confessed with great penitence and many tears, and although he could not support himself on his feet, yet, being sustained in the arms of his servants and friends, he devoutly received the Holy Sacrament, while thus out of his bed. The king, who was accustomed frequently and affectionately to visit him, came immediately afterwards to his room, and he, causing himself out of reverence to be raised up, sat in his bed describing his malady and the different circumstances connected with it, lamenting, besides, that he had offended God and man, inasmuch as that he had not laboured in art as he ought to have done. He was then seized with a violent paroxysm, the forerunner of death, when the king, rising and supporting his head to give him such assistance and do him such favour as he could, in the hope of alleviating his sufferings, the spirit of Leonardo, which was most divine, conscious that he could attain to no greater honour, departed in the arms of the monarch, being at that time in the sixty-seventh year of his age."

Rembrandt was another painter whose complete devotion to religion is revealed in all his work. All his life Rembrandt found great delight in portraying Bible scenes. Some of these pictures are amongst the most famous in the world and are found in great museums in many lands. Among the best known are: "Saint Paul in Prison," "The Supper at Emmaus," "Samson's Capture by the Philistines," "Saint Peter Among the Servants of the High Priests," "Christ Disputing with the Doctors in the Temple," "The Good Samaritan" and "The Flight into Egypt."

He had that temperamental difficulty in handling money so often found in men of genius. Although a man of simple tastes and frugal habits, he was lavish in expenditure. When he wanted anything connected with his work, he was generous to a fault. The high prices commanded by his pictures gave him ample means for a time. The readiness with which he earned money caused his generosity to become extravagance with the result that he was frequently in serious financial difficulties and at one time was imprisoned for debt.

The death of his first wife and of his child, together with his mental troubles, had a disquieting effect upon the painter. A biographer writes: "The master withdrew more into himself. In his grief and disappointment, he accepted solitude and misunderstanding, and grew more and more a power unto himself, regardless of the adverse thoughts of non-sympathisers and rivals. He turned for comfort to the Bible, as had been his wont in all the main events of his life. 'The Marriage Feast of Samson' and 'Belshazzar's Feast' memorialised his own nuptial festivities. Various Holy Families, 'The Carpenter's Household,' 'The Meeting of Elizabeth and Mary,' 'Manoah's Prayer,' expressed his own hope of offspring.

"He tasted popularity and success, and knew their worth; he put worldly ambition into the balance with his ambitions as an artist, and found it wanting. When the supreme trial of his spirit came; when, like Job, he suffered the loss of wife, children, home, and worldly possessions; when his allegiance to his ideal was put to a final test, he was not found wanting. He testified to his belief in it until his last breath, for in his spiritual need lay his greatest strength." [2]

In his picture: "Christ at Emmaus" he caught, to an extraordinary degree, the intense situation when the eyes of the two men who had gone in to sup with Jesus were opened as he took bread and blessed it and gave it to them. The wonder and worship in their eyes is unforgettable and speaks with eloquence to every understanding heart.

Other great pictures of Rembrandt are: "Annunciation to the Shepherds"; "The Adoration of the Shepherds"; "Jesus Blessing Little Children"; and "The Descent from the Cross." These paintings and many others show how completely and lovingly he gave his whole powers to the interpretation of

---

[2] Elizabeth A. Sharp, *Rembrandt*, pp. 127 and 170.

Christ's life and work. The late Dr. R. P. Downes, for many years Editor of *Great Thoughts Magazine,* paid this tribute to Rembrandt: "If anyone wishes to know what the common people in Holland and Germany did actually believe in the sixteenth century concerning the Gospel of Jesus Christ, he must go, not to the Synods of Dort, or to the writings of Lutheran or Calvinistic divines, but to the works of Rembrandt. We learn from this great artist that the common people, whom he loved and represented, heard Jesus Christ gladly. They knew and felt sure that Jesus Christ was the poor man's Saviour and the poor man's friend, and they treasured up his words and listened to the story of His works with reverence and affection. It was on the life of Christ, in His relation to the common people, that the genius of Rembrandt spent itself in its finest intensity."

The French artist, Gustave Doré, is chiefly remembered because of his illustrations of Biblical themes, yet he was in his fortieth year, and already famous, before he produced "Christ Leaving the Prætorium," the first of his many Scriptural pictures.

The subject was suggested to him by Canon F. K. Harford, an Anglican clergyman and artist whom Doré had met in Paris. A warm and enduring friendship sprang up between the two but when Harford urged Doré to turn his attention to Biblical themes the latter had misgivings. "Although a Catholic I am not an orthodox Christian," he said. Then opening the New Testament at First Corinthians, chapter thirteen, he read, slowly and impressively, Paul's great hymn of love: "That is my religion," he said, "a religion of love."

Canon Harford said that the dramatic moment showing Christ leaving the Prætorium, just before he took up the Cross, had never been pictorially treated and after a while Doré agreed to attempt it. The work was begun in 1867 but not completed until 1872. When first completed Harford objected that the colors were too bright and Doré agreed that his friend was right. In an hour he obliterated the hard work of several months, but it was well worth while for when it was finally produced with its darkened sky, its grim realism and impressive tragedy were instantly recognized.

For the remainder of his life Doré concentrated chiefly on religious subjects. To tens of thousands he became the "painter-preacher." His absorption in his work was amazing, sometimes for months he could think of nothing else than the work engaging his attention. This absorption had marked effects upon his character; always reverent he became a man of deep religious feeling.

Two things greatly saddened him; the outcome of the seige of Paris in 1870 and the death of his mother. After the former event it was said that he became a changed man, all brightness and laughter seemed to go out of his life. He found his consolation in work and in religion.

On the day of his mother's burial in Paris, March 16, 1881, he wrote the following letter to Canon Harford:

"Dear Friend—She is no more. I am alone. She is dead my mother, so tender, so deeply venerated; dead after a long and cruel agony; and this morning, a few hours hence, I shall carry her to her last resting-place. I am without force, my friend, and do not know how to submit myself to that hard law which spares none of us. It seems that a black, unbridgeable gulf yawns before me. You are a priest, my friend, I conjure you, then, send up all your prayers to heaven for the repose of her dear and sainted soul, and for the sustainment of my own reason; for I am singularly overpowered by despair, discouragement, and fear of the future."

The great English artist, Holman Hunt, frankly declared that it was the deliberate aim of all his art to glorify Christ. To an intimate friend he wrote: "My desire is very strong to use my powers to make more tangible Jesus Christ's history and teaching. Art has often illustrated the theme, but it has surrounded it with many enervating fables and perverted the heroic drama with feeble representation. We have reason to believe that the Father of all demands that every generation should contribute its own quota of knowledge and wisdom to attain the final purpose. I wish to do my poor part, and in pursuing this aim I ought not surely to serve art less perfectly." [3]

Hunt's famous picture, "The Light of the World," now to be seen in St. Paul's Cathedral, London, is probably the best known picture of modern times, because of the countless reproductions of it. Other pictures by Holman Hunt are: "The Triumph of the Innocents"; "Finding of the

---

[3] H. W. Shrewsbury, *Brothers in Art*, p. 42.

Saviour in the Temple"; "The Shadow of Death," a scene in the carpenter's shop at Nazareth; and "The Scapegoat."

Holman Hunt left an interesting account of how he came to paint the famous picture "The Shadow of Death." This painting represents Jesus as a boy, standing in His father's carpenter shop, stretching out His arms as though He were tired. On the wall behind Him is His shadow strangely prophetic of the time, when in a similar position, He was to be nailed to the cross. The peevish criticism of some "Is not this the carpenter's son?" arrested Hunt's attention.

He began to wonder what the thoughts of Mary were during the long years when Jesus lived in obscurity. The glorious promises of the Annunciation were painfully slow in being fulfilled. How natural that from time to time she should rehearse all the wonderful happenings that had attended Christ's birth; that she should examine with proud and loving interest those royal gifts brought years before by the Wise Men from the East—the golden crown, the sceptre, the kingly raiment—and strengthen her tested faith by gazing upon these marvellous memorials. Then the terrible shock when the first forebodings came to her heart that a very different crown and kingdom was His portion; the awakening up of a presentiment of coming tragedy and the anguish that would rend her heart. By an extraordinary flash of genius Holman Hunt interpreted an intensely dramatic phase of the life of Jesus and Mary.

The American painter, Benjamin West, will be remembered as the creator of the pictures "The Death of Wolfe," and "Penn's Treaty with the Indians," but his enduring fame will probably rest upon his famous picture "Christ Healing the Sick." Born in Pennsylvania in 1738, in what was then the backwoods of America, Benjamin West's career reads like a romance. As a child of seven he had sketched a remarkable likeness of his baby sister who had been left in his keeping. From that day until the time forty-seven years later when he succeeded Sir Joshua Reynolds as President of the Royal Academy of Arts, a position he held until his death in 1820, he ranked as the greatest of American artists and one of the foremost painters of the world.

West was a Quaker and a man of deep religious feeling. His occupation as a painter caused some misgivings among the straightest of the Quaker faith. To some it savored of vanity that a member of their society should give himself up to follow decorative art. Very solemnly they called a meeting to discuss the question. His extraordinary gifts none could deny and when one of their number arose and declared that undoubtedly Benjamin's artistic ability was a gift from God, they solemnly approved his calling. Members placed their hands upon his head and, in a sort of ordination service, prayed for God's blessing upon him in his career as a painter. West never forgot that solemn hour and devoutly fulfilled their prayerful wishes.

When his great picture, "Christ Healing the Sick," was hung in the Royal Academy in London there was placed alongside of it, the tiny picture West had made in his father's garret with his first box of paints. He is buried in St. Paul's Cathedral.

The list of great painters who have combined unusual artistic ability with tender and reverent devotion is a very long one. In *Christianity and Culture,*[4] John G. Bowran writes: "Many of the world's most famous painters devoted their lives to religious studies and particularly to the portraiture of the Divine Man, God's Son, Redeemer of mankind. The world's greatest artists have been fascinated by Jesus. Many of them were keen students of the gospels and the personality of Jesus enthralled them. They lived with His glorious figure in their minds and they spent their lives in revealing and displaying them. On the canvas they taught what their eyes saw and what their hearts felt of the truth as it is in Jesus.

"Each artist was an evangelist and a preacher. There is every possible difference in their conceptions, but they are at one in their noble desire to set forth His fame and His praise. Many of them had a living and personal love for the Saviour and their art was the means by which they proved their loyalty and their devotion. And Christianity throughout their lives was an unfailing inspiration. It is marvellous how these great preachers of the brush and pencil never wearied in following Christ and in paying Him homage. It is the simple truth that these artists came to the highest excellence in their culture because they were students in the school of Christ and concentrated their talents to His glory.

"It is impossible to name them all but these names are honoured in the highest courts of Art, and they were all

---

John G. Bowran, *Christianity and Culture,* p. 69.

famous because of their absorption in Christ, in His ministry and work. Leonardo da Vinci, Albert Durer, Raphael, Correggio, Veronese, Rubens, Van Dyck, Rembrandt, Murillo, Gustave Doré and many others. In more modern times these great names are recalled: Munkacsy, Holman Hunt, Burne Jones, Dante Gabriel Rossetti, John Everett Millais, G. F. Watts, Sir Noel Paton, Madox Brown, and hosts of others have been Evangelists of Art."

CHAPTER THREE

Religious Faith of Great Authors

SIR WALTER SCOTT was another great figure in English literature whose religious faith remained undimmed throughout life. "In the autobiographical notes which Scott made at Ashestiel, he gives a none too favourable account of the Sundays of his boyhood: 'The discipline of the Presbyterian Sabbath was severely strict, and I think injudiciously so. Although Bunyan's *Pilgrim,* Gesner's *Death of Abel,* Rowe's *Letters,* and one or two other books, which, for that reason, I still have a favour for, were admitted to relieve the gloom of one dull sermon succeeding to another—there was far too much tedium annexed to the duties of the day; and in the end it did none of us any good.' His mother, however, was of a less stern disposition, for 'she joined to a light and happy temper of mind a strong turn to study poetry and works of imagination. She was sincerely devout, but her religion was, as became her sex, of a cast less severe than my father's.'" He had the passage, "The Night Cometh," engraved upon his sundial, as Dr. Samuel Johnson had upon his watch. He wanted to remind himself that noonday is constantly wearing on towards evening and life must be taken seriously.

"Scott's debt to the religion of his home was real and

lasting. No man knew his Bible better than he did, and its influence upon his thought and his writings was profound. And he got that love of the Book of books in the George Square home, and imbibed much of his wide and detailed knowledge of the Scriptures in his boyhood days. Both in the *Journal* and the *Familiar Letters* he constantly quotes the Bible, and the novels show how thoroughly he was impregnated with its spirit. It was his life-long companion." [1] He had tender regard for troubled souls, as all his novels reveal, but he had no patience with cynical scorn. He wrote:

> "And better had they ne'er been born,
> Who read to doubt, or read to scorn."

His novels are replete with references to religion and all such are characterized with deep reverence. Students of Scott's life know how wave after wave of serious trouble broke over him until at times he seemed to be numb and staggered with the blows. After the death of his wife, he almost despaired. "God knows," he said, "I am at sea in the dark." Yet he writes: "I will not be dethroned by any rebellious passion that may raise its standard against me. I want to finish my task and then—good night." With magnificent fortitude Scott met repeated blows; poverty, bereavement, calumny, but he never faltered, or, if he did, it was but for a moment. "If anywhere in another world," says Mark Rutherford, "the blessings which men have conferred here are taken into account in distributing reward, surely the

---

[1] John A. Patten, *Sir Walter Scott*, p. 151.

choicest in the store of the Most High will be reserved for His servant Scott! It may be said of others that they have made the world wise or rich, but of him it must be said that he, more than all, has made the world happier—wiser too, wiser through its happiness."

When death was near, he said to his son-in-law, Lockhart: "I have but a minute to speak to you. My dear, be a good man, be virtuous, be religious, be a good man. Nothing else will give you any comfort when you come to lie here."

Lockhart, who became Scott's biographer, thus describes the closing scene in the life of the great novelist: "Sir Walter desired to be moved through his rooms in the bath-chair. We moved him leisurely for an hour or more up and down the hall and the great library. 'I have seen much,' he kept saying, 'but nothing like my ain hoose—give me one turn more.' Next morning he desired to be drawn into the library and placed by the central window, that he might look upon the Tweed. Here he expressed a wish that I should read to him. I asked him what book. He said, 'Need you ask? There is but one.' I chose the fourteenth chapter of St. John's Gospel." When Lockhart had finished reading, he said, with deep devotion, "That is a great comfort."

Charles Dickens has an honoured place as a writer in English fiction. Perhaps no other man so skillfully blended comedy and tragedy, humour and pathos in his work, and made his characters so familiar to the world. He criticised hypocrisy severely and poured such savage contempt upon shams that some have misunderstood his attitude to genuine religion. No careful reader of his books could possibly fail to recognize his acceptance of the fundamental teachings of Christianity. "I know that, but for the mercy of God," he wrote, "I might easily have been, for any care that was taken of me, a little robber and a little vagabond." There is not a novel from his pen that is not emphatically Christian in tone and viewpoint. Just one year before his death, when writing to his own son, he said: "Try to do to others as you would have them do to you, and do not be discouraged if they should fail sometimes. It is much better for you that they should fail in obeying the greatest rule laid down by our Saviour than that you should. I put a New Testament among your books because it is the best book that ever was, or ever will be, known in the world, and because it teaches you the best lessons by which any human creature who tries to be truthful and faithful to duty can be guided."

"Nothing could be more poignant and pathetic than the words he places in the lips of the dying prisoner in Chancery: 'I hope my merciful Judge,' he gasps, 'will bear in mind my heavy punishment on earth. Twenty years my friend— twenty years in this hideous grave! My heart broke when my child died, and I could not even kiss him in his little coffin. My loneliness since in all this noise and riot has been dreadful. My God, forgive me. He has seen my solitary, lingering death.' "

On the occasion of the Dickens centenary in 1909 there appeared in *Faith and Life,* a French Protestant magazine, an article evidently written by a distinguished Roman Catholic, who said: "Dickens was a Christian certainly, but

of what denomination? may we ask curiously. Catholic or
Protestant? Ritualist or Evangelical? To this question his
biographers give no definite answer. For my part, I consider
that any response would tend to falisfy our idea of the religion of Dickens. The truth is that his Christianity embraces
all denominations, in this sense, that he admits their common
dogmas, and does not expressly reject any one of them. It
is founded entirely upon one book, the New Testament, or,
to speak with exactitude, upon a part of this book. But this
part constitutes the essential and universal element, the Sermon on the Mount, completed by the parables. It has often
been said that the doctrines of the Sermon on the Mount
animate the entire work of Dickens, and, in fact, the truth
reveals itself to every reader from 'Oliver Twist' to 'Great
Expectations.' " [2]

In a tragic passage in *Little Dorrit,* when the darkened
soul of Mrs. Clennam is battling with doubt and fear, Dickens
puts these beautiful words into the mouth of little Dorrit:
"Be guided only by the healer of the sick, the raiser of the
dead, the friend of all who were afflicted and forlorn, the
patient Master who shed tears of compassion for our infirmi-
ties. We cannot but be right if we put all the rest away, and
do everything in remembrance of Him. There is no vengeance
and no infliction of suffering in His life, I am sure. There
can be no confusion in following Him, and seeking for no
other footsteps, I am certain."

William Makepeace Thackeray, contemporary of Dickens,

---

[2] *Great Thoughts,* Volume III, Series VII, p. 259.

gave to English literature six of its greatest novels. These are: *Vanity Fair, Pendennis, The Newcomes, The Virginians, Henry Esmond* and *Denis Duval*. In some respects, at least, his writing has never been excelled.

Thackeray sustained a heavy blow when his young wife suffered a mental breakdown from which she never recovered. The experience made him even more gentle and sensitive—if that were possible. He was so versatile that he did not settle down to writing very early in life, a dozen paths seemed open to him and he was scarcely known when, at the age of thirty-six, he wrote *Vanity Fair*

Few writers of fiction have made more frequent or more effective use of the Bible than Thackeray. The great, colorful, dramas of Scripture exerted a profound influence upon him which he was glad to acknowledge. Writing of Thackeray's last and unfinished novel, a biographer says "The whole of *Denis Duval* is in the tone of this passage. For pure and elevated thought; for serene faith; for the conviction that no good is ever lost; that life, at heart, is both right and beautiful: in all these respects this magnificent fragment towers above the novels of its time like the central peak of a great range. It is pleasant to know that Thackeray's greatest rival appreciated this wonderful fragment, that Dickens said of it: 'In respect of earnest feeling, far-seeing purpose, character, incident, and a certain loving picturesqueness blending the whole, I believe *Denis Duval* to be much the best of his works.' " [3]

---

[3] Nathaniel Wright Stephenson, *The Spiritual Drama in the Life of Thackeray*, p. 190.

"I like to think," he once said, "that my books have been written by a God-fearing man. Their morality—the vanity of everything but love and goodness—is but a reflection of the teaching of our Lord." Toward the close of his life, Thackeray's faith became increasingly clear and strong. An intimate friend was about to leave England and the famous novelist did not expect ever to see him again. "I shall not see you again," he said, "but look in that book and you will find something which, I am sure, will please and comfort you." Writing about this some years later, this friend said: "It was a prayer that he might never write a word inconsistent with the love of God or the love of man; that he might never propagate his own prejudices or pander to those of others; that he might speak the truth with his pen, and that he might never be actuated by a love of greed. I particularly remember that the prayer wound up with the words, 'For the sake of Jesus Christ our Lord.' "

There is less ground for claiming Robert Louis Stevenson as an orthodox Christian than some others written of in this book. As a child he had poor health and throughout life —he died at forty-four—he lived under a shadow because of this physical condition. He pursued happiness with passionate zest and all his books are a plea for cheerful living. He declared: "As I live I feel more and more that literature should be cheerful and brave spirited, even if it cannot be made beautiful, pious and heroic. The Bible in most parts is a cheerful book; it is our piping theologies, tracts, and sermons, that are dull and dowrie."

On many religious matters he was a "devout agnostic." Nevertheless when in the South Seas religion occupied his attention. Occasionally he taught in Sunday school; he was in sympathy with the missionaries and family prayers were observed in his unusual household there. "The *Prayers* which he wrote for use at Vailima were part of the mixed service which he was wont to hold there. The rest was made up in the reading of the Bible in the Samoan language by his stepson. Hymns were sung in Samoan, and the prayers were as we have them, or sometimes extempore. They inculcate the duty of cheerfulness and mutual help: 'For our sins forgiven or prevented, for our shame unpublished, we bless and thank Thee, O God'; and again, 'that we may be true to what small best we can attain'; also he prays for the grace of courage. 'Thy guilty innocents,' he names himself and his household, again a paradox, not unnatural, and one not difficult to understand. The service concluded with the Lord's Prayer in Samoan, 'that sublime prayer of the Christians,' says Balzac. . . . R. L. S. would certainly have said he believed in God, but he would have refused any definition or explanation; he would have said 'I cannot tell,' which is the agnostic answer to all questions. His morality was the morality he was taught in his youth, purged of conventional or merely adventitious elements, with particular stress laid on the maxims that inculcated courage, cheerfulness, and kindness. But as he did not hold or continue to accept the theological doctrines he had first imbibed, he would have been hard put to it to give reasons for such faith as was in him. He postulates maxims of conduct as self-evident truths,

or which upon reflection are entitled to rank as proving themselves. And here I leave this interesting but dubious subject." [4]

One might expect from a sick man a certain measure of
morbidness not untinged with bitterness and doubt. There
is no bitterness in any of his books, and where there is doubt
it is reverent and eager to hope. As life wore on, he came
increasingly to believe in what he calls "the kindness of the
scheme of things and the goodness of our veiled God." His
parents were deeply religious and while Stevenson differed
from them in many ways, it evidently gave him great pleasure
to be able to write these lines to his father: "There is a fine
text in the Bible, I don't know where, to the effect that all
things work together for good to those who love the Lord
. . . strange as it may seem to you, everything has been, in
one way or the other, bringing me a little nearer to what I
think you would like me to be. . . . 'Tis a strange world,
indeed, but there is a manifest God for those who care to
look for him."

Over forty years ago, the literary critic, W. T. Stead,
wrote of Leo Tolstoy: "He is the most notable man of
letters now living. There is no Russian so famous; and,
outside Russia, there is no literary personality so conspicuous.
His novels are read everywhere, in every language; his ideas
attract the attention of everybody who thinks. He has been
a soldier, a man of the world, a student, a recluse, a vision-

---

[4] Francis Watt, *R. L. S.,* pp. 278 and 281.

ary, and a reformer. He is at once a great genius, a consummate artist, and a religious apostle."

The story of Tolstoy's life is that of an earnest seeker after God. As a boy he had some faith which he lost. When he left the University of Kazan, at the age of eighteen he had given up belief in anything he had ever been taught. "He entered upon his manhood, having left for ever behind him, as he thought, the traditional religion, assuming too that most of the people round about him, as a matter of fact, were in the same position. There is, however, a wide gulf between Tolstoy and the average careless person. He was *conscious* that he had abandoned the old faith. It was, as we shall see, the void left within him by the removal of the old pieties and sanctions for life, which became in his case the seat, first of his spiritual misery, and at last the beginning of his hope. He entered manhood free from dogmatic bondage, but at the same time with a more or less active belief in God, or rather a kind of feeling for God." [5] Then for many years he sought, passionately and often in despair, to find an anchorage for his soul, and, at last, when he was fifty years of age, faith came and his life was changed. Writing of this experience, he says: "My whole life underwent a sudden transformation. Everything was completely changed." From that hour until the close of his life Tolstoy became a sort of literary evangelist. "Up to the time that this great change came into his life," writes A. C. Turville, "his was a heart that knew no rest. He tried everything, yet nothing for long. But

---

[5] J. A. Hutton, *Pilgrims in the Region of Faith*, p. 118.

from the moment of his great change he never deviated. All that he had previously dreamed of goodness, purity, peace and love flashed upon him with all the force of a revelation from the picture of Jesus in the gospels. Christ made his aspirations tangible."

Nevertheless his recovery of faith did not mean his return to the Greek Orthodox Church nor his acceptance of much which most Christians believe. "Tolstoy was finally turned away from the church not by rational objections to its doctrines but by moral objections to its practices. He was shocked by its exclusiveness, by its denunciation of Catholics, Protestants, and Russian sectarians and dissenters as people living in spiritual darkness. This was indeed opposed to the Christian precept of brotherly love. On the pretence of preserving in all its purity the Greco-Russian Orthodox faith, the church was merely seeking the best means of performing in the sight of men certain human obligations (the sacraments). Worse than this was the church's attitude towards war, and in particular towards the war between Russia and Turkey of 1877-78; and towards capital punishment, and in particular towards the execution of certain revolutionary agitators in the times immediately following this war." [6]

In 1883 he composed a summary of his creed in semi-autobiographical form to which he gave the name, *My Religion*. It should be remembered that many of the positions taken in this book he later modified and in some cases aban-

---

[6] G. R. Noyes, *Tolstoy*, p. 218.

doned altogether. His convictions about the essential truths of the Christian religion deepened with the passing years but he was often inconsistent and when he believed he did so fiercely. He believed in the underlying unity of all true spiritual experience and the love of God, as taught by Jesus, increasingly laid claim upon him. In 1901 he was excommunicated from the Russian Church and the surprise is that this had not taken place earlier as his repeated attacks upon the Church had become more bitter.

It is not easy to define his attitude towards Jesus but, as G. R. Noyes points out, while "He never says directly that Jesus was inspired or infallible, yet he assumes for his teaching an infallibility he does not assert. When he has once determined to his own satisfaction the original teaching of Jesus, he accepts it with reverent faith." It would appear as though he reserved the right to determine what in the New Testament he believed to be Christ's teaching and to reject what did not appeal to him. "Taking as his foundation the simplest and most intelligible portions of the text, he interprets the rest in accord with them. Passages that seem to him false or hopelessly obscure he either rejects as interpolations or boldly alters, sometimes, though not always, fortifying himself by the comparison of manuscripts or by the use of the lexicon."

When he wrote *My Religion* he was definitely opposed to the doctrine of personal immortality, yet in a letter written to his wife fifteen years later (1898) he said: "I rode home through Turgenev's wood. . . . And I thought, as I think continually, of death. And it became so clear to me that it will be just as good, though in a different way, on the other side of death, and I could understand why the Jews represented paradise as a garden. The purest joy is the joy of nature. It was clear to me that there it will be just as good —no, better. I tried to call forth in myself doubt of the other life, such as I used to have, and I could not as I could before, but I could call forth confidence within me."

Tolstoy was always and everywhere a seeker, a spiritual pilgrim. His writings and his life witness to the soul's spiritual hunger. His greatest contribution to humanity was not the development of an ethical system but his frantically honest attempt to apply to modern life the world-renouncing ethics of Jesus.

A modern critic, writing of the message of that great French novelist, Victor Hugo, says: "Victor Hugo's *Les Miserables* represents the first attempt in fiction to show that if sin dims the divine image, conscience disturbs the soul with sore discontent, while Christ never despairs of making bad men good, but toils ever on until publican and outcast alike stand forth clothed with every courage, every heroism, every virtue, being of goodness all compact."

Victor Hugo is one of the greatest literary figures of all time. He was a strange, erratic, turbulent genius, sometimes coarse, often extravagant and always theatrical, but never dull. His father was an officer in the army of the French Republic and an ardent Napoleonist. His mother's sympathies were with the Royalists. "His early years were years of wandering, for Napoleon was then advancing through

Europe in his might as a conqueror, and the child followed with his father and mother the steps of that dark archangel of war. From Besançon to Marseilles, from Marseilles to Elba, from Elba to Paris, from Paris to Avellians, where he played at the foot of Vesuvius; thence to Spain, and finally to Paris again—he was perpetually on the move. In one of his earlier odes he tells us that his cradle had often rested on a drum, that water from the brook was brought to his childish lips in a soldier's helmet, and the tatters of some worn-out battle-flag had been wrapped round him in his sleep. It is not difficult to realize how the imagination of the ardent boy was tinctured by these scenes of his early life."

Hugo cared little for the opinion of others and had scant regard for ordinary conventions. Madame Duclaux writes: "He was a man of genius, freed from the bondage of accepted opinion, having long outlived one creed and conviction, he looked at life through no eyes but his own, went his own way, nor cared to follow other men's examples."

Hugo's quarrels with the Church were violent—he was always violent—and final. Previous to his death in 1885, at the age of eighty-three, he had written in his will: "I believe in God. I refuse the service of all the Churches; I beg a prayer from every soul."

A series of misfortunes which visited Hugo in middle life, together with acute distress in domestic relations, left him stunned. Many of his poems, often deeply religious and frequently sad, reveal how much he suffered and endured. "There is more irony than faith so far in the poet's resignation. He accepts the rod, but cannot say with Dante: 'In Thy

will lies our peace.' Still the progress of the poems shows
the gradual exhaustion of despair, the submission of a broken
heart. Renouvier was right when he said that Victor Hugo,
in his youth a Christian from habit and custom; after 1830,
a Christian in language, but not in thought; became spon-
taneously and unconsciously a real Christian at the epoch of
the *Contemplations,* although a Christian heretic—a gnostic
or a Manichee. He never found it out, and, to the end of
his days, had no inkling of the nature of a religion which he
considered the original result of his own meditation." [7]

Hugo drew great inspiration from the reading of the Gospel narratives. "His virtuous thieves and angelic prostitutes
are, after all, but the transposition into modern art of figures
sufficiently familiar in the Gospels. Hugo was as intimately
convinced as any priest that the heart of man is complex,
never wholly good or wholly bad, and that there is no sin
which may not be redeemed.

"M. Paul Stapfer, in his personal recollections of Victor
Hugo, records the following monologue which fell from the
lips of the poet in an after-dinner conversation. 'How poor,
how small, how absurd,' he said, 'atheism is! God exists.
I am more sure of His existence than I am of my own. If
God lends me sufficient length of life I want to write a book
showing how necessary to the soul prayer is—how necessary
and how efficacious. Personally, I never pass four hours
without prayer. I pray regularly every morning and evening.
If I wake in the night I pray. What do I pray for? Strength.

---

[7] Madame Duclaux, *Victor Hugo,* p. 194.

I know what is right and what is wrong, but I realize my imperfections, and that of myself I have not the strength to resist evil. God surrounds and upholds us. We are in Him. From Him we have life, movement, being. All is created by Him. But it is not true to say that He has created the world. He creates it unceasingly. He is the Soul of the Universe.' " [8]

With amazing unanimity *Les Miserables* has been given first place among great novels. It is a deeply religious story. The wide, far-reaching mercy of God and the soul's ability to reach up and grasp God's right hand and hold on to it constitute the background of this monumental tale. The book tells, in terse, dramatic form, the story of man's recoverability. It exhibits the worst man as having something within him which no injustice can extinguish; and it is to this divine element that Christianity appeals. The closing words of Jean Valjean to Cosette and Marius indicate what was Hugo's own faith: "My children, remember God is above. He sees all. He knows all He does, amid His great stars. Remember God is love." A few minutes later, ere his soul passed out, Jean whispered: "My children, I can no longer see very clearly. Think of me a little. I know not what is the matter with me but *I see light.*"

A recent biographer of Sir James Barrie does not hesitate to say that Barrie is "In our time the finest embodiment of Scotland's national genius." Like his fellow-countrymen, Burns and Carlyle, Barrie was born in a peasant's cottage. He first saw the light in the little village of Kirriemuir in

---

[8] R. P. Downes, *Hours with the Immortals,* p. 299.

1866, a village he was afterwards to make immortal under the name of Thrums. After taking his Master of Arts degree at Edinburgh University, Barrie secured a position on a Nottingham newspaper and afterwards went to London where he worked as a free lance journalist. His articles were soon appearing in the leading London magazines. When these articles were re-published in book form, it was evident that a writer had arisen with a gift of genius all his own. His books, *My Lady Nicotine; When a Man's Single; Auld Lichte Idylls; A Window in Thrums; The Little Minister* and *Peter Pan,* are known the world over and most have been read by millions.

After his triumph as an author Barrie achieved even greater success as a playwright. This is all the more amazing when it is remembered that when he wrote his first plays, he did so without the slightest knowledge of the technique of the stage and without any idea, apparently, that such a thing existed. It has often been said that his plays broke every law ever held by dramatic critics yet the spectators laughed or were in tears by turns. "The wizard waved his wand and they were mesmerized."

Like a great many writers of his day, Barrie has been decidedly critical yet his criticisms have been written with such deep sentiment and whimsical wisdom that he has endeared himself even to those against whom his thrusts have been made. Life to him is a glorious adventure and he leaves the impression that death too will equally be an adventure.

In his book, *Margaret Ogilvy,* one of the most gracious tributes ever paid by a son to a mother, one finds this pungent passage which contains much self-revelation: "When you looked into my mother's eyes you knew, as if He had told you, why God sent her into the world—it was to open the minds of all who looked to beautiful thoughts. And that is the beginning and end of literature. Those eyes that I cannot see until I was six years old have guided me through life, and I pray God they may remain my only earthly judge to the last. They were never more my guide than when I helped to put her to earth, not whimpering because my mother had been taken away after seventy-six glorious years of life, but exulting in her even at the grave." [9]

In May, 1892, an event made an impression on Barrie which drew from him one of those very rare expressions of his emotion and his religious views. His youngest sister, Margaret, was engaged to be married to a young clergyman. Three weeks before the time appointed for the wedding, this young minister was thrown from a horse and killed. Not only was the young man betrothed to his sister, but he was one of Barrie's most intimate friends and the author wrote a letter to the congregation at Bower, where the clergyman had been minister, with the request that it be read from the pulpit. Here is an excerpt from the letter:

"To you, at the grave of him who was in three weeks' time to become her husband, my sister sends her love. She has not physical strength to be with you just now in body, but she is with you in spirit, and God is near her, and she is not afraid. You are her loved ones, for it was you who,

---

[9] J. M. Barrie, her son, *Margaret Ogilvy*, p. 5.

under God, called him to Bower, and gave him the manse to which he was about to bring her, and, as he loved you, she loves you. God, who gave his Son for the redemption of the world, has told her that He had need of the disciple's life also, and that he died to bring his people of Bower to God's knees. So God chose His own way, and took her Jim, her dear young minister, and she says, God's will be done; and she thanks Him for taking away so suddenly only one who was ready to face his Maker without a moment's warning. His great goodness, she says to you, in not taking some one who was unprepared, is her comfort, and should be yours. And she prays that Mr. Winter's six months' ministry among you, and his death among you while doing his duty, has borne and will continue to bear good fruit. And always she will so pray, and she asks you to pray for her. And she says that you are not to grieve for her over-much, for she is in God's keeping." [10]

Nathaniel Hawthorne, who was frequently referred to as the most distinguished craftsman of the New England School of Letters, did not reach fame until the age of forty-five. He wrote *The Scarlet Letter*. His romances are written within a narrow range and deal with a grim Puritan past that both fascinated and repelled him. In his introduction to *The Scarlet Letter* he writes of his first New England ancestor, Major William Hathorne (it was Nathaniel who inserted the "w"), a stern man who became a magistrate in his day. Concern-

---

[10] J. A. Hammerton, *Barrie, The Story of a Genius*, p. 173.

ing him Nathaniel wrote: "The figure of that first ancestor, invested by family tradition with a dim and dusky grandeur, was present to my boyish imagination as far back as I can remember. It still haunts me, and induces a sort of home-feeling with the past, which I scarcely claim in reference to the present, phase of the town. I seem to have a stronger claim to a residence here on account of this grave, bearded, sable-cloaked and steeple-crowned progenitor—who came so early, with his Bible and his sword, and trod the unworn street with such a stately port, and made so large a figure as a man of war and peace—a stronger claim than for myself, whose name is seldom heard and my face scarcely known. He was a soldier, legislator, judge; he was a ruler in the church; he had all the Puritanic traits, both good and evil. He was likewise a bitter persecutor, as witness the Quakers, who have remembered him in their histories, and relate an incident of his hard severity towards a woman of their sect which will last longer, it is to be feared, than any of his better deeds, though these were many."

Nathaniel Hawthorne was profoundly interested in ethical questions. The problem of sin had for him a great fascination. That he revolted against the Puritan teaching of the past day and indeed against the traditional view he had been taught as a boy, is without question. Nevertheless, Hawthorne had profound religious convictions. He refused to accept any iron-bound dogma and his church affiliations were slight. He believed, however, in divine providence and though he did not set out to be a teacher of morals, as some have assumed, every one of his books show how his mind dwelt on the moral significance of conduct. He died on the morning of May 12, 1864, at the home of his friend, Franklin Pierce in Plymouth. A few days after his death his widow wrote this beautiful tribute to the memory of her husband: "Everything noble, beautiful, and generous in his action Mr. Hawthorne hid from himself, even more cunningly than he hid himself from others. He positively never contemplated the best thing he could do as in the slightest degree a personal matter; but somehow as a small concordance with God's order—a matter of course. It was almost impossible to utter to him a word of commendation. He made praise show absurd and out of place, and the praiser a mean blunderer; so perfectly did everything take its true place before him. The flame of his eyes consumed compliment, cant, sham, and falsehood, while the most wretched sinners—so many of whom came to confess to him—met in his glance a pity and sympathy so infinite, that they ceased to be afraid of God, and began to return to Him. In his eyes, as Tennyson sings, 'God and Nature met in Light.' So that he could hardly be quarrelled with for veiling himself from others, since he veiled himself from himself. His own soul was behind the wings of the cherubim—sacred, like all souls which have not been desecrated by the world. I never dared to gaze at him, even I, unless his lids were down. It seemed an invasion into a holy place. To the last, he was in a measure to me a divine mystery; for he was so to himself. I have an eternity, thank God, in which to know him more and more, or I should die in despair. Even now I progress in knowledge of him, for he informs me constantly." [11]

The literary reputation of General Lew Wallace rests on three historical romances: *The Fair God, The Prince of India,* and *Ben Hur,* an absorbing tale of Christ. This last novel has been translated into a score of languages and has provided and continues to provide entertainment on stage and screen.

Lew Wallace was born in Brockville, Indiana, in 1827, and his early life was singularly free from religious influence. When still quite young he abandoned law business to recruit for the Mexican War. Later he entered the Civil War and saved Washington from almost certain capture at the battle of Monocacy. In 1865 he returned to law and was made Governor of New Mexico during 1878-81 and was Minister to Turkey in 1881-85.

He began to write Ben Hur in 1876. In order to study the period previous to and immediately following the birth of Christ, he spent fully four years in a thorough examination of every form of literature that would serve his purpose. He had no convictions about the person or mission of Christ and so brought to the subject a mind free from prejudices, favorable or otherwise. In an interview granted to Doctor O. S. Marden he said: "I was in quest of knowledge, but I had no faith to sustain, no creed to bolster up. The result was that the whole field of religious and biblical history

---

[11] Julian Hawthorne, *Nathaniel Hawthorne and His Wife,* Volume II, p. 352.

opened up before me; and, my vision not being clouded by
previously formed opinions, I was enabled to survey it without the aid of lenses. I believe I was thorough and persistent.
I know I was conscientious in my search for the truth. I
weighed, I analyzed, I counted and compared. The evolution from conjecture into knowledge, through opinion and
belief, was gradual but irresistible; and at length I stood
firmly and defiantly on the solid rock.

"Upward of seven hundred thousand copies of 'Ben Hur'
have been published, and it has been translated into all languages from French to Arabic. But, whether it has ever
influenced the mind of a single reader or not, I am sure its
conception and preparation—if it has done nothing more—
have convinced its author of the divinity of the lowly Naza-
rene who walked and talked with God." [12]

The death of the famous English novelist, Arnold Bennett,
together with the publication of his journal, has made that
outspoken and fearless writer a subject of much comment.
He was often frankly—almost savagely—opposed to organized religion. The drab side of religion, its negations and
frequent intolerances, as he saw it in youth, repelled him and
all his life he seemed to enjoy holding up to ridicule phases
of religion with which in his boyhood he had been more or
less familiar.

Shortly after his death, his wife published a biography of
him in which she states clearly her own impressions of his
attitude to religion: "Religion had no inspiring effect on

---

[12] O. S. Marden, *How They Succeeded*, p. 251.

Arnold Bennett. Though saturated in his youth with the beautiful religion of Christ, his intellect refused to be impressed with it. His heart (though he was kind-hearted) rejected systematically all trace of religious impulse—yet at heart he was a Christian. When he ever gave me a chance to imagine he was fighting with himself not to appear a Christian, I would immediately say to him, 'Don't pretend to yourself, my dear, at heart you are more of a Christian than many who pose as such.'

"I have often thought that his unreligious attitude was a garment to protect himself from being accused of being sentimental—for religion teaches not only to be kind at heart but to show our feelings, to express them, to talk about eternal peace, eternal felicity, to idealize everything for the glory of God and the joy of man." [13]

From the pen of Arnold Bennett we have his views concerning religion. A few years ago the London *Daily Express* obtained from a number of distinguished persons, their religious opinions; Arnold Bennett was one of the group. He wrote: "Is there a God? Call this phenomenon a First Cause, a Supreme Being, a Creator—what you like; God is a good name for it. I believe that there is a God, if only for the reason that I can imagine no other explanation of a marvellous, scientifically-ordered, and law-controlled universe. This argument is called 'the argument from design,' and it presents itself to me as a pretty good argument. But what may be the attributes of God, and His ultimate aim, I have

---

[13] Marguerite, his wife, *My Arnold Bennett*, p. 8.

not the slightest idea. And I do not exercise my brain in trying to decide what His aim is, because I feel that my brain is utterly unequal to so sublime a problem, and could not possibly solve it. Why should I agitate myself over a matter which exceeds my mental powers? I do not agitate myself.

"There is, however, another argument for the existence of God which, for me, is more cogent even than the rather physical argument from design—namely, that in every one of us is a force which we call conscience, a force which tends always in the direction of justice, mercy, and kindness. Nobody is without a conscience; the conduct of nobody is entirely uninfluenced by his conscience. The universality of conscience, together with the broad uniformity of its influence on conduct, convinces me far more satisfactorily than anything else that it must have been implanted in us by a Creator Who had a clear aim (whatever that aim may be) in the creation and slow evolution of His universe. I got this idea many years since from Tolstoy's *Anna Karenina,* and it has never left me." [14]

He also stated very clearly his views on the Bible: "Dogmatic Christianity is based on the Bible, and on the Bible alone. And the Bible has proved to be very unsure ground for dogma, as it was bound to prove as soon as the bias of religious tradition was eliminated from the study of it. The Bible is not a book. It is, as somebody recently very well described it, an anthology. As a whole, it is a body of great

---

[14] *My Religion,* pp. 9 and 10.

literary value and of much moral value. The best books in
it are, perhaps, supreme in their kind. But of the divine
origin of any of these books no proof (in my opinion) has
yet been brought forward which reaches the standard of
demonstration demanded by historical students in secular
fields of inquiry."

While not accepting orthodox views concerning Christ, he
repeatedly expressed his admiration for one whom he considered unique among moral teachers: "It seems to me that
Christ better than anybody understood the secret of happiness, which is the avowed end of all religious beliefs. Christ
taught an all-embracing sympathy. He taught humility, meekness. He taught us to judge not that we be not judged. He
taught forgiveness. He taught the return of good for evil.
In a word, his religion was, in practice, the religion of kindli-
ness."[15] "The moral teaching of Christ makes a most powerful appeal to me, and I should not care to assert that in the
field of morals Christ was not the greatest man that ever
lived."

Concerning the problem of a future life, Mr. Bennett
wrote: "On a balance of probabilities I am inclined to accept
the theory of a future life; and I am fairly sure that, if
indeed there is a future life, my conduct in this present life
will materially affect the nature of it. Further than this I
do not go, cannot go, and do not wish to go."

---

[15] *Ibid.*, p. 10.

CHAPTER FOUR

Religious Faith of Great Merchants

ONE of the great British merchants of last century was Sir George Williams, who will ever be gratefully remembered as the founder of the Young Men's Christian Association. He migrated to London when a mere youth, without influence or capital, yet within a comparatively short time, by unusual business qualities, he took his place as one of the leading merchant princes of Great Britain.

The Nineteenth Century was one of unusual prosperity for Great Britain, but even then fortunes were not accumulated without close application and industrious habits. He himself had an extraordinary faculty for hard work and this he combined with deep religious sincerity. He lived in a time when many business concerns looked somewhat cynically, if not superciliously, on the religious devotions of employees. Sir George Williams said over and over again that—all other things being equal—the men of God make the best business men. He held the firm conviction that a Christian man in business had, in his religion, a decided asset.

The head of a great commercial concern is seldom a hero to his employees, but the transparent sincerity and deep religious convictions of Sir George Williams stamped him as one of the most winsome personalities of his generation, and nowhere was he more popular than with his own employees. Once, when he was very ill, an employee who was thrown into daily contact with him wrote: "I have known him intimately these many years. I see him, not merely every day, but almost every hour of the day and many times in the hour. I have seen him in touch with men of all classes and conditions, and it is my sober thought that I shall never see his like again." [1]

Sir George believed in personal evangelism. He spoke to all who came in close contact with him about his religion in the most natural and frank manner, and his interest in the spiritual welfare of people was beautiful and sincere. His religion was not something which peered out occasionally. It penetrated his whole life and was the background of all his thinking. On his frequent voyages across the Atlantic he made a point of speaking to everyone on the entire ship, from fireman to the chief officers, and whenever possible he spoke about religious matters, and such was his kindly and gracious manner that there is no record of anyone having resented his approach.

He was one of the first merchants to introduce in his establishment a daily religious service. The employees were invited, and such was the character of these services that an aggressive missionary society was formed in the establishment and many young men were led through these services to become active in Christian work. It was his custom, each day after lunch, to meet with groups of men engaged in

---

[1] J. E. Hodder Williams, *The Life of Sir George Williams*, p. 41.

Christian work for consultation and prayer, and it will never
be fully known just how widespread and generous were his
gifts. In his room hung a motto: "God First," and few men
have lived up to such an ideal as he did. He was a merchant prince; at the same time he was a king in the realm of
spiritual affairs.

"George Williams was to the end strict, stern, positive in
his religious beliefs. He belonged to the old Evangelical
school of thought, and he held to its creed with intensity and
intense sincerity. But his heart was so great, his charity so
broad, that the austerity of his doctrine was covered by the
gracious mantle of kindness and sympathy. Sympathy could
never have produced the Young Men's Christian Association, Calvinism could never have produced the Young Men's
Christian Association. But these two, peace and the sword,
love of the sinner and hatred of the sin, were welded and
fused in the steadfast and loving heart of George Williams,
who clung with fierce tenacity to the rigorous doctrines of the
guilt of man and the wrath of God, but was so full of pity
that under most bitter provocation he would think no evil,
and was ever seeking for the face of goodness behind the
mask of sin." [2]

The life of William Hesketh Lever, famous English merchant, reads like a romance. He was born in 1851 at Bolton
where his father was a shop-keeper in a very small way.
For several years the lad helped his father sweep floors, clean
windows, deliver parcels and wrap up soap. While in his

[2] *Ibid.*, p. 245.

early twenties, he launched out in business as a soap manufacturer, and the growth of his enterprise is one of the business romances of the last fifty years. He selected fifty acres on the banks of the river Mersey, near Liverpool, and there began to build an immense factory and a village which is now known the world over as Port Sunlight. Since the village was first opened in 1890, thousands of social workers and reformers drawn from nearly every country on earth have visited Port Sunlight and Lever's enterprise has received world-wide praise.

Following a number of other merchants who took seriously their responsibility for the welfare of their employees, Lever instituted a plan of profit sharing by which all employees could invest their savings with the firm and share in its success. At the present time over twenty thousand employees are co-partners in the firm holding stock in the company to the value of over fifteen million dollars.

William Lever was made a baronet in 1911. He was created Lord Leverhulme in 1917, and in 1921 Viscount Leverhulme. The pressure of business made it difficult for Leverhulme to be a very close student, but he was a man with varied interests. In religious matters he had been brought up a Congregationalist and had the strong independent views of that denomination. He held important positions as a layman in his church, but had pronounced views which he did not hesitate to say on many matters relating to religion. When visiting Egypt, for instance, he was much impressed with many of the ethical values of Mohammedanism and aroused the ire of Christian missionaries by some of his criticisms of their work. In his diary at the time, he wrote: "It appears clearer than ever that the money spent on missionary efforts is worse than wasted; that the same money spent in taking the little children out of the gutters of England, feeding, clothing and educating them decently until they are fifteen, then putting them in respectable service or the Colonies, would do ten thousand times more good."

Leverhulme never became an enthusiastic supporter of foreign missions, but in latter years he was willing to support the programme of a missionary society provided that it was always accompanied by a practical programme of general education and training in handicrafts and industrial pursuits.

"Leverhulme was a Christian with decided Liberal tendencies, generous in support of those Christian activities which seemed to him thoroughly practical in character. Religious argument he knew to be the bitterest form of controversy and he scrupulously avoided it. He had respect for all sincere forms of belief. His outlook was that of the Theological student at Longfellow's *Wayside Inn,* who—

> '. . . Preached to all men everywhere
> The Gospel of the Golden Rule,
> The new Commandment given to men,
> Thinking the deed and not the creed,
> Would help us in our utmost need?' "

He had great veneration for the Bible and read a portion of it every day. He loved it as literature and valued it as a book of practical advice. The Bible, in his judgement, was not indispensable because of its sacrosanct character, but because human experience has proved it to be sound. He believed that the Sermon on the Mount was not a collection of abstract idealisms, but practical economic laws as universal in their application as the law of gravitation. "If a man has not read the book of Proverbs," he once said in the course of an address, "I will never believe that he can be a true, careful, sound and cautious man." [3] While he was not a Puritan, at the same time he opposed drinking, betting and gambling and considered them foolish and indefensible.

In the early fifties of last century an Irish youth reached Canada who although poor and almost friendless at the time was destined to become the country's greatest merchant. Indeed, to such success did this young Irish immigrant attain that his biographer, George G. Nasmith, said that he had probably achieved the greatest commercial success in the history of commerce in Canada. After some experience in outlying places, Timothy Eaton moved to Toronto when it had a population of less than ten per cent of what it has today. By indomitable perseverance and restless energy combined with rare willingness to try out new methods, he built up a business which, at the time of his death in 1907, was by far the greatest concern of its kind in the Dominion. His first newspaper advertisement appeared on December 8, 1869, when he announced that in connection with his business, goods would be sold for cash only and furthermore there would be one fixed price for everything. This announcement was greeted with amusement and not a little ridicule. The

[3] By his son, *Viscount Leverhulme*, p. 275.

system of bartering and exchanging goods had existed so long that no one seemed to think that a business could succeed by other methods. Many predicted that in a few months the business would fail, others limited its existence to a few weeks.

Considering the times in which he lived, Timothy Eaton showed amazing progressiveness and consideration for employees. He introduced the Saturday half holiday, much shorter hours for employees and better working conditions generally. He manifested throughout his life anxious concern and sympathetic interest in all his work people. Born in humble circumstances, himself one of nine children, fatherless from his birth, by his honesty, consideration for others and energy, he left an example which has inspired thousands of young Canadian lads. He did what is probably the most difficult of all things, namely, he became a nation's most successful merchant and at the same time retained the respect and admiration of his employees and his business rivals. He was a man of deep religious convictions and it would be hard to say whether he was more interested in his business or in the building up of church life. He was foremost in every enterprise which had for its object the well-being of the people. Today a beautiful church in Toronto stands as a memorial of him.

He died on the last day of January, 1907, and the entire city, which had known him for nearly half a century, paid extraordinary tributes to his memory. The following eulogy taken from the Toronto *Mail and Empire* was one of many similar articles that appeared in the press at that time:

"A good man. That was Timothy Eaton. God's good man. There is a perfume attaching to the name and life of such a man not to be reached by those whom only Fame has crowned. Mr. Eaton was necessarily a great man. The result of his vast business enterprises shows that, but there was something so thoroughly good, clean—one might say, holy—in the whole life of the great merchant prince, something so lovable in his quiet, reticent way of doing good, something so wonderful in the steadfastness with which he wrought from nothing a great fortune, that you come back to the word good—a good man which sums it all up.

"He 'made good' in his fight with this world, honestly and uprightly; and in an age when business men are apt to go to pieces and end a long life in disgrace, it is small wonder that we should point with pride to such a man as Timothy Eaton, and be fired with a desire to try to do as he did, to live soberly, sanely, wisely; to pursue our business earnestly and honestly; to hold fast to a saving religious faith, letting infidelity and 'free' thought, this fad and that, go by.

"It was a beautiful life; a beautiful death. They say he looked as one who already knew the heavenly peace and rest. He will long be mourned and never forgotten, and I doubt not when Patrick's Day comes many a shamrock will find its way to where the grand old Irish-Canadian lies at rest."

There is a striking similarity between the careers of Sir George Williams and Sir William Hartley. Both men were born in humble circumstances and by unusual diligence in business and ambitious endeavor rose to positions of impor-

tance in the business world. Both were men of deep religious conviction and sought to apply religion, to the conduct of their business. It is with this aspect of their lives
that we are concerned in this book.

William Hartley became a manufacturer of jam and when
thirty years of age found himself owner and director of a
large business concern. Branches of his rapidly expanding
business were opened in different places and within a few
years there were several thousand employees in his service.

Hartley viewed with some concern the development of his
business. Not only was he a member of the Methodist Church
but he was an active worker in the Sunday school and a lay
preacher. Regarding his religious training and his own position, this is what he says: "I never remember a time in my
life when I had not a real genuine desire to serve the Lord.
My father and grandfather were both local preachers, and
when I was a small boy, I often accompanied my father to
his country appointments and also into his pulpit. I have
given out a hymn many a time when I was a small boy. At
that time I had an honest desire to be a local preacher, but
this was frustrated. When I was about twelve or thirteen
years of age it was decided to have a harmonium in the
chapel at Colne, my native town, and it was the earnest wish
of my parents, especially my mother, that I should learn to
play; and with some financial strain they placed me under a
music teacher and purchased a small harmonium for my use
at home, with the sole and only object of my officiating at
the instrument in the chapel. I have this harmonium now in
my house. My idea of being a local preacher was of neces-

sity completely abandoned owing to my duty at the harmonium. . . . I was organist in the Colne chapel for sixteen years until I was twenty-eight." [4]

Hartley knew that no amount of church activity or lavishness in giving to benevolent enterprises could ever be a substitute for what he believed to be the Christian way of doing business. There was at that time in England (the eighties and nineties of last century) a growing social consciousness which was extremely critical of all big manufacturing concerns such as Hartley's. There and then he decided to make a move which placed him among the pioneers of movements making for better conditions.

He instituted the plan of sharing profits with his employees. He paid wages which exceeded from twenty to forty per cent those paid by his competitors in the same district and, in addition, after seventeen years he had distributed profits amounting to one hundred and seventy-five thousand dollars. He felt that the interests of his employees were identical with his own and that they had a claim to share in the prosperity of the business. He was constantly on the look-out for schemes to make work pleasanter and one of his favorite maxims was that work should be made attractive to the worker.

After his London factory had been in operation for some time, the *Croydon Chronicle* made this comment: "Of course the requirements of modern life are such that a great deal of work has to be done by machinery; but, to the credit of Mr.

[4] A. S. Peake, *The Life of Sir William Hartley*, p. 34.

Hartley be it said, he has seen that his men have become the masters of the machines instead of their slaves, and thus has made of industrialism a blessing and not, what it is in many cases, an unmitigated curse." [5]

He was elected President of the Primitive Methodist Conference in 1909, a position he graced with charm and dignity. Loyal churchman though he was, he had little patience with religious controversy. His biographer Professor A. S. Peake says, "He would probably have agreed with Matthew Arnold that conduct was three-fourths of life, except that he might have urged that this proportion was far too small." He put his position before the Conference in these words: "I am not one of those who are much troubled as to creed; but I am *much* exercised as to whether I am such a disciple of Jesus Christ that my work-people, my business friends, my neighbours, and my family can constantly see the spirit and temper of the Master in my actions.

"My own opinion is that for thirty-five years (this being the time of my recollection) we have listened to too many doctrinal and theological sermons and too few as to the absolute importance of living Christlike lives; and unless we be actually miniature Christs day by day, breathing His spirit and living His life, it matters not what we believe, for our religion is a sham. Our actual creed is what we put into practice, and no more; and we want to be careful to see that our practice is equal to our creed." [6]

In a frank and vigorous address delivered to an audience

---

[5] *Ibid.*, p. 52.
[6] *Ibid.*, p. 223.

of working men in Nottingham, he said: "Religion is not only a thing of the church, the prayer meeting, or holiness conventions; it is all these but a very great deal more. It is a thing of the factory, the workshop, the mine, the office; in a word it is a life to be lived."

The United States has been singularly fortunate in having many great merchants who combined business interest with deep religious conviction and high ideals of Christian living. In no other country in the world have there been so many men who arose from poor circumstances to positions of eminence and great influence. John Wanamaker is a good illustration of this. Born in a humble home on the outskirts of Philadelphia in 1837, he lost his father when he was fourteen, and had to make his own way in life. So enthusiastic was he in supporting the Young Men's Christian Association that he was appointed to be the first salaried secretary of the Philadelphia branch. He remained in that position for seven years, then, with very small capital, he entered business for himself. The phenomenal growth of his business is one of the most thrilling stories of business life. In some respects the great concern he built is unequalled in the world. Throughout the prosperous years—prosperous to an extent that would have swept some men off their feet—John Wanamaker maintained high Christian ideals, and ever regarded himself as a steward of God. From the very beginning of his career he took a keen active interest in Sunday-school work. "Mr. Wanamaker gave many glowing tributes to the helpful influence of the Sunday school upon him and of its value in general. In 1920, to the World's Sunday School Convention at Tokyo, he wrote: 'I became a member of a country Sunday school when a boy ten years old and have been a member continuously for seventy-three years. I regard the Sunday school as the principal educator of my life. Through the Holy Scriptures, the Bible, I found knowledge not to be obtained elsewhere, which established and developed fixed principles and foundations upon which all I am and whatever I have done were securely built upon and anchored.

" 'As a boy, so far as I know, I was not religiously inclined. With copper coins, which I worked for, I bought my first little Bible from my Sunday school teacher. It told me that there was a God and how the world was created and that the attributes of God were justice, mercy, love, and truth, and that injustice, selfishness, cunning, jealousies, dishonesties, and falsehoods of human nature had never brought permanent success to individuals or nations. I *believed* what I read in the Bible. . . . In a little mission Sunday school of the Lutheran Church I bought from my teacher a small red leather Bible, about eight inches long and six inches wide. This Bible cost two dollars and seventy-five cents, which I paid for in small installments as I saved up my own money that I had earned.

" 'Looking back over my life, that little red Bible was the foundation on which my life has been built, and it has made possible all that has counted most in my life. I know now that it was the greatest and most important and far-reaching purchase I have ever made; and every other investment of

my life seems to me, after mature years, only secondary.' "
It would be impossible to enumerate his benefactions to
Christian work. He was active in opposition to evil and
naturally he made enemies, but few questioned his sincerity.

John Wanamaker, undoubtedly in the front rank of the
world's merchant princes, was first of all a Christian. "It
was his warm and unquestioning religious faith that was at
the foundation of his life. It was this all pervading, ever-
present principle that made him the man of service he was,
and beautified all his efforts and achievements. Not nar-
rowed by sect or creed, but with a religion that comprehended
all humanity, he carried into all his activities the teachings of
the Master whom he had served." [7] He was Superintendent
of the Bethany Sunday School in Philadelphia for over forty
years. When he began there were only two teachers and
twenty-seven pupils. Recently the school reported a mem-
bership of four thousand five hundred, and it is one of the
best managed Sunday schools in the world. Mr. Wanamaker gave to the work of the Church and Sunday school
the very best of which he was capable.

The career of the American merchant George Peabody
had in it all the dramatic appeal that the public loves so much.
Leaving school with only the rudiments of an education he
secured employment in a village store and was thus able to
augment the income of a much harassed mother. Some
years afterwards he commenced business for himself and at

---

[7] Russell H. Conwell, *The Romantic Rise of a Great American*, pp.
11 and 195.

the age of thirty-five he was at the head of a flourishing business.

He removed to London, England, where he established a mercantile and banking business and became an outstanding figure in the financial life of that great city. He is remembered chiefly because of his remarkable adaptability to the ways of a new country and for his whole-hearted support of every benevolent enterprise. He literally gave millions for the support of educational projects both in England and in the United States. His total gifts exceeded nine million dollars.

By his generosity the Peabody Institute was built at his birthplace, Danvers in Massachusetts. He was on a visit to America when it was opened and in reply to an address of appreciation read to him by the Governor of Massachusetts on that occasion he said: "Though Providence has granted me unusual success in the pursuit of fortune in other lands, I am still in heart the humble boy who left yonder humble cottage many years ago. There is not a boy within the sound of my voice whose opportunities and advantages are not greater than were my own, and I have achieved nothing that is impossible to the humblest boy among you. Remember, however, that in order to be truly great it is not necessary that you should gain wealth and importance. Be true, be steadfast, be fearless, be honest; keep your record clean and pure, for these are the only things that make men really great."

After the impressive memorial service for Peabody, held in Westminster Abbey, Rev. Newman Hall, D.D., one of the most distinguished divines of his generation, said: "It is a fearful responsibility to die rich, after a life of covetousness which is idolatry. All honour to George Peabody, that, in his lifetime he recognized his responsibility, as well as enjoyed the privileges of wealth; and that he derived greater satisfaction in scattering his possessions amongst the poor than in indefinitely augmenting his store."

George Peabody was one of the first wealthy men to voice, over and over, his sense of responsibility for the distribution of the wealth which he earned. When giving two million dollars for education in the Southern States, he wrote, "I feel most deeply that it is the duty and privilege of the more favored and wealthy portions of our nation to assist those less fortunate, and I wish to discharge, as far as I am able, my own responsibility in this matter. . . . I make this gift with reverent recognition of the need of the blessing of Almighty God upon this gift, and with the fervent prayer that, under His guidance, your counsels may be directed for the highest good." [8]

William E. Dodge was another great merchant whose religious life suffered no eclipse when riches came. He was the product of a Christian home, and when a mere boy he solemnly dedicated his life to God, and splendidly kept his promise. Early in his career he began to teach in Sunday school and his interest in the pupils led him to keep in close touch with them during the week.

He was one of the organizers and most generous sup-

[8] Hanaford, *Life of George Peabody*, p. 157.

porters of the Young Men's Christian Association in the
United States. He was elected President of the National
Temperance Society and was characterized by Dr. Theodore
L. Cuyler as, "The most catholic representative of the temperance reform in all its phases and activities." When a
congressman at Washington he held emphatic views on moral
questions yet he was never intolerant and always held, to
an astonishing degree, the deep respect of his political opponents. "Personal activity in religious effort was habitual with
him and his connection with religious societies such as The
American Bible Society, city missions, and Sunday schools
was by no means nominal."

For many years he had to do a great deal of travelling,
but those who came into contact with him bore witness to his
gracious influence and his immutable Christian testimony.
When he began to make money he set aside a definite proportion for religious purposes. As his income grew he increased his gifts. He was interested in young men of
modest means who were preparing for the work of the
Christian ministry and more especially those men whose early
educational advantages had been somewhat meagre. In this
way he gave much needed assistance to scores of men. During the Civil War he was honored with the friendship of
Abraham Lincoln and was actively interested in the work of
the National Christian Commission, whose object was to
look after the wounded and provide for the religious needs
of the soldiers. He was elected a representative to Congress and became a very effective speaker.

Merchant, statesman, philanthropist, William E. Dodge

was first and foremost a humble Christian. He died in 1883, and his death was widely mourned.

The death of Arthur Nash of Cincinnati some years ago brought to public attention one of the most sincere attempts of modern times to apply Christian principles to business life. As owner of the Nash Clothing Company he announced his intention of applying the Golden Rule to business and even the most cynical admitted his transparent sincerity.

One of his sons enlisted in the Canadian army and was seriously wounded at Vimy Ridge. Like thousands of other professing Christians, Arthur Nash was shaken out of complacency with the accepted tenets of modern civilization and particularly with organized religion. "What is wrong with our religion," he asked himself a score of times, "look at what men are doing to each other in Europe—and they are practically all so-called Christian nations. Cannot the religion they profess stop this butchery?"

A clergyman with whom he discussed the matter invited him to address a meeting in his church and in order to do this Mr. Nash studied the New Testament carefully. One result of this was he became convinced that if organized religion seemed to be ineffective in dealing with war, neither was it a potent influence in the business world.

He was deeply impressed with the Sermon on the Mount; especially the words "Therefore all things whatsoever ye would that men should do unto you, do ye even so unto them; for this is the law and the prophets." "As I read that verse," he said, "the light of its true meaning broke upon my soul. I laid down the Bible and said, 'The only thing that is wrong with Christianity is that we are not giving it a trial.' " So in preparing an address which was to have dealt exclusively with Christianity and War, he was led into another field equally significant, Christianity and Business.

"The years that followed Mr. Nash's decision brought to him all manner of severe tests for this rule of Jesus. The production of the little factory was doubled and even trebled, and the profits were increasing accordingly. Here right away was a test of Mr. Nash's own sincerity. What should be done with these increased profits? Should he quietly put them away in his own bank account? Why should he not? Had he not already increased the wages of his workers far above the standards of other factories? And yet the Golden Rule said, 'As ye would that men should do unto you.' Arthur Nash decided that those profits must be shared with the men and women who had helped to create them. A meeting of the employees was called and the whole matter discussed. It was finally voted that after interest charges were paid on the original investment, the profits still remaining should be equally divided between Mr. Nash and the workers in his factory. At first those who had been receiving the highest wages got the larger share of this bonus. But at the request of the skilled workers themselves, it was later arranged that the poorer and less skilled workers should receive more. It was agreed that 'they need it more.' " [9]

The significance of the attempt was not lost upon the em-

---

[9] Harold B. Hunting, *Pioneers of Goodwill,* p. 135.

ployees. An amazing change came over the whole concern. The output of work greatly increased and workers began to love their tasks. Some called it their church, and weddings were solemnized there. Noon-day prayer meetings were organized, and one of the most frequent and fervent prayers was: "Thy will be done in this factory as it is done in heaven." The removal by death of Arthur Nash in the fall of 1927 marked an experiment which must be registered as truly sincere as it seemed spectacular.

CHAPTER FIVE

Religious Faith of Great Musicians

JOHANN SEBASTIAN BACH has been called the founder of modern music. He was born at Eisenach in Germany, March 15, 1685, and when fifteen years of age began
the study of the organ. He became the greatest master of
compositions for this instrument and one of its greatest
players. A biographer writes: "He was unaffectedly pious,
without any of the scruples that induced his ancestor to leave
Hungary and he wrote both for the Lutheran Church—to
which he belonged—and also for the Church of Rome. His
tastes were extremely simple and he loved the society of his
family. He disregarded the honor which awaited him everywhere and he lived, composing, teaching, and playing; advancing his art in all he did."

As a composer of religious music he has had no equal.
"The idea conveyed by many of his cantatas and choruses is
that of a people kneeling in respectful adoration before a
celestial being, or the cry of men glorifying God in the in-
comparable beauty of His creations. Nowhere in the domain
of art is the grandeur of religion more worthily celebrated
than in the sacred compositions of Bach." His contemporaries and successors are unanimous in their unqualified
praise of his work. His greatest sacred work, *The Matthew*

Passion, probably has no rival in the realm of sacred music. He held strong religious views but his zeal never made him intolerant. "Bach's place in Lutheran Church history is very important. He is connected with the Reformation through the choral which Martin Luther used so much as a means of spreading the new views of religion. Bach was a strict Lutheran and the choral, or hymn to be sung by the congregation was perhaps the most important expression of Lutheran religious feeling." [1]

Increasingly Bach felt it to be his mission in life to improve church music. His whole being was exalted under its spell and he expressed his views in these words: "The sole object of all music should be the glory of God and pleasant recreation."

George Frederick Handel is a fine example of those who have combined intense religious feeling with passionate devotion to music. His best works all had religious themes. His oratorio, *The Messiah,* which must have thrilled countless audiences, has well been called "The most glorious musical biography of Jesus in the possession of men." Its tremendous appeal never fails, and it came from the soul of a musician who was amazingly sensitive to religious feeling.

"Handel possessed an inexhaustible fund of melody of the noblest order; an almost unequalled command of musical expression; perfect power over all the resources of his science; the faculty of wielding huge masses of tone with perfect ease and felicity; and he was without rival in the sublimity

---

[1] C. F. A. Williams, *Bach,* p. 94.

of ideas. The problem which he so successfully solved in the oratorio was that of giving such dramatic force to the music, in which he clothed the sacred texts, as to be able to dispense with all scenic and stage effects." [2]

After his decision to devote himself to sacred music, Handel did his most effective and enduring work. He believed implicitly that nothing less than the inspiration of God made his work possible. When asked what his feelings were when composing *The Messiah,* he said: Whether in the body or not, I cannot tell." When he wrote the passage beginning "He was despised," Handel was completely overcome with emotion and friends found him in tears.

Although born in Germany, Handel spent most of his life in England, where he became such a favorite that his every appearance in public was the signal for a great ovation. He often expressed the wish that he might die on Good Friday in the hope of soon meeting his Lord and Saviour on the day of His resurrection. The musician's wish was granted. He died on Good Friday, 1759, and was buried in Westminster Abbey.

The great Austrian composer, Mozart, once said: "I have such a sense of religion that I shall never do anything that I would not do before the whole world."

In some respects Mozart was the greatest genius in the history of music. His amazing precocity as a child—he began to take lessons in his fourth year—excited astonishment everywhere. In his sixth year he played before large audi-

---

[2] John G. Bowran, *Christianity and Culture,* p. 93.

ences in Munich, Vienna, Paris and London. His subsequent career fulfilled the promise of his early years. In spite of his tragic death at the early age of thirty-five, he wrote eight hundred musical compositions, comprising eighteen operas, forty-nine symphonies, fifteen overtures and over seventy pieces of sacred music. His cantatas bear witness to his intensely religious spirit and his attitude to matters of religion is clearly expressed in his own words: "Friends who have no religion cannot long be my friends."

He sustained a number of crushing blows which undoubtedly saddened him but deepened his faith. Mozart's mother died at Paris on July 3, 1778. On the night of her decease he wrote to his father's intimate friend, the Abbé Bullinger: "My dear Friend,—Sympathise with me on this the most wretched and melancholy day of my life. I write at two o'clock in the morning to inform you that my mother—my dearest mother—is no more! God has called her to himself, I saw clearly that nothing could save her, and resigned myself entirely to the will of God; He gave, and He can take away. Picture to yourself the state of alarm, care, and anxiety in which I have been kept for the last fortnight. She died without being conscious of anything—her life went out like a taper. Three days ago she confessed, received the sacrament and extreme unction; but since that time she has been constantly delirious and rambling, until this afternoon at twenty-one minutes after five, when she was seized with convulsions, and immediately lost all perception and feeling. I pressed her hand and spoke to her; but she neither saw me, heard me, nor seemed in the least sensible; and in this state she lay for five hours, namely, till twenty-one minutes past ten, when she departed, no one being present but myself, M. Haine, a good friend of ours whom my father knows, and the nurse.

"I cannot at present write you the whole particulars of the illness; but my belief is that she was to die—that it was the will of God. Let me now beg the friendly service of you, to prepare my poor father by gentle degrees for the melancholy tidings. I wrote to him by the same post, but told him no more than that she was very ill, and I now await his answer, by which I shall be guided. May God support and strengthen him! Oh, my friend! through the especial grace of God I have been enabled to endure the whole with fortitude and resignation, and have long since been consoled under this great loss. In her extremity I prayed for two things: a blessed dying hour for my mother and courage and strength for myself; and the gracious God heard my prayer, and richly bestowed those blessings upon me. Pray therefore, dear friend, support my father. Say what you can to him, in order that when he knows the worst, he may not feel it too bitterly. I commend my sister also to you from the bottom of my heart. Call on both of them soon, but say no word of the death—only prepare them. You can do and say what you will; but let me be so far at ease as to have no new misfortune to expect. Comfort my dear father and my dear sister, and pray send me a speedy answer. Adieu. I remain your much obliged and grateful servant." [3]

---

[3] Edward Holmes, *The Life of Mozart*, p. 121.

Mozart bore the blow, which was extremely severe to one with so sensitive and affectionate disposition, with magnificent fortitude. On the same day that he wrote to the Abbé Bullinger, shortly before his mother died, he sought to console his stricken father by a letter which breathed tender solicitude and deep religious faith. He wrote: "They want to give me hope; but I have not much. I have been long already—for days and nights together—between hope and fear; but I have now entirely resigned myself to the will of God, and I hope that you and my dear sister will do the like. What are the means then to give us calm and peace, in a degree, if not absolutely? I am resigned, let the end be what it may, because I know that God, who, however mysteriously he may proceed to human eyes, ordains everything for the best, so wills it; and I am not easily persuaded out of the belief that neither physician nor any other man, neither misfortunate nor accident, can either take or give life, but God alone, though these are the means which he mostly employs; but even these not always. We see people constantly sinking and dying around us; but I do not say, on that account, that my mother must and will die, or that we have lost all hope. She may recover if it be the will of God. I, however, find consolation in these reflections, after praying to God as earnestly as I am able for my dear mother's health and life; they strengthen, encourage, and console me, and you must needs think I require them. Let us now change the subject, and quit these melancholy thoughts. Let us hope, if not much, and put our trust in God, consoling ourselves with the reflection that everything is well ordered which the Almighty orders, and that He best knows what is essential to our temporal happiness and our eternal salvation." [4]

The famous Hungarian pianist and composer, Franz Liszt, was always deeply interested in the religious and political movements of his day. He made his first public appearances in his ninth year and his genius was at once recognized. His association with musicians, however, disillusioned him; every day he listened to men and women whose stark materialism disgusted him. His religious impulses became so strong that he thought of entering the priesthood and he opened his heart to his father who was annoyed as well as astounded: "You belong to art and not to the church," said his father and he promptly removed every religious book from the boy's room.

A few years later, after a bitter disappointment in love, Franz once more sought to take holy orders. He called upon his confessor, the Abbé Bardin, flung himself at his knees and begged to be allowed to enter a religious order. The priest was not easily moved and he felt sure the petulant mood was not a permanent one; "Come, my child," he said lifting him up, "you must serve God and the church in your profession as an artist without aspiring incontinently to the sublime virtues of the priesthood."

It was the Abbé Lamennais who convinced Franz Liszt that, for him, service to God meant devotion to a musical career for which he was so eminently fitted. "Franz became deeply attached to this great, vehement spirit. He

---

[4] *Ibid.*, p. 123.

learned from him that the work of the rarest artists is their lives. He learned the philosophy of music, the priestess of the art; he learned that, like the sentinels of the Lord, he must henceforth watch, pray and strive, day and night. Was not the Eternal Geometrician the greatest virtuoso, since his work was the world? Thence it followed that the laws of creation were the same as those of art and that beauty was identical with life. To know and to understand the work of God was the object of science; to render it in its material or sensible aspects was the object of art. 'Art for art's sake is an absurdity. The perfecting of the creature whose progress it manifests is its aims.' But its roots did not strike down merely into the powers of men; it was united to God through love. Art was therefore never either haphazard or disorderly; its real discipline was poetry, its method excellence. It had no limitations, since it was the very thing that God had most deliberately left unlimited: a progression, a development. The highest duty of the artist was to furnish the divinity with modes of expression that were perpetually new." [5]

As a pianist Liszt played like an inspired poet; at the same time he was one of the world's most prolific composers. Handsome in appearance, gentle in manner, Liszt attracted women as he was drawn to them. He insisted that only a love romance could kindle his musical genius and in this his friend, Richard Wagner, concurred. Some of these romances shocked even the Parisians of his day and his irregularities

---

[5] Guy De Pourtalès, *Franz Liszt,* p. 35.

were a frequent source of agitation to him and of embarrassment to his friends.

Throughout his long and brilliant career he remained loyal to the Roman Catholic Church; often for months he attended mass daily and observed the strictest practices of the church. After the death of Caroline d'Artigaux, mother of three of his children, he wrote: "How could I help withdrawing at once into meditation and prayer when I learned of the death of Caroline d'Artigaux? She was one of the purest manifestations of God's blessing upon earth. Her long sufferings, endured with so much Christian sweetness and resignation, had ripened her for heaven. There she enters at last into the joy of the Lord—she had no concern with that of this world, and the Infinite alone was worthy of her heavenly soul. Blessed be God for having recalled her from her earthly exile, and may her intercession obtain for us the grace to remain united to him."

He was much devoted to the writings of Pascal and one day, after reading this favorite author, he wrote in the margin of the book what probably was a clear statement ot his religious views: "If it were established that all the metaphysical proofs in support of the existence of God were reduced to nothing by the arguments of philosophy, would still remain One, absolutely invincible. The affirmation of God through our lamentations, the need we have for Him, the aspiration of our souls towards His love: this suffices for me, and I do not have to ask for it to remain a believer to the last breath of my life."

For thirteen years Liszt lived at Weimar with the Princess

Sayn-Wittgenstein. They wished to marry but there were difficulties, ecclesiastical and political, and when in 1860, it seemed that the obstacles to the marriage were insurmountable he wrote: "I am mortally down-hearted, and can neither say anything nor hear anything. Prayer alone helps me at moments, but alas, imperatively as I need it, I cannot pray any more with much continuity. May God give me the grace to pass through this mortal crisis, and may the light of his pity shine through my shadows."

In 1865 Liszt joined the Franciscan Order and became henceforth the Abbé Liszt. He still received pupils—gratis —and occasionally gave concerts at which his popularity was, if anything, greater than ever. Towards the close of his life he was honoured with the canonry of Albano and this present from the church evidently gave him pleasure. He said: "The idea of outward advancement was as strange as possible to me. I was only following, in all simplicity and honesty of heart, the old Catholic tendency of my youth. If I had not been opposed in my first fervor by my dear good mother and my confessor, the Abbé Bardin, it would have led me to the seminary in 1830 and later into the priesthood. One reasons at random on the ideal. I know nothing loftier than that of the priest meditating, practising and teaching the three theological virtues, faith, hope, charity, voluntarily sacrificing his life, crowned with martyrdom when God grants it! Would I have been worthy of such a vocation? Divine grace alone could have made it possible. As it is, the loving tenderness of my mother and the prudence of the Abbé Bardin have left me in great danger from temptations which I have been able to resist very inadequately. Poetry, music and also some grain of native revolt have too long subjugated me."

Liszt died at Bayreuth, on July 31, 1886, in his seventy-fifth year.

When the calamity of deafness came upon the great composer, Ludwig van Beethoven, he said, not without bitterness: "For thee, poor Beethoven, no happiness may be expected outside thyself. Thou wilt have to create everything within." This extraordinary man was eccentric in the extreme, and was shut up within his own world not only because of his deafness but on account of his genius. One of his early teachers complained of him in despair: "He will never do anything as other people; he never learns to do anything according to rule."

But whatever else is true of this solitary man—solitary in life as in death—for at his funeral "no wife, no son, no daughter wept at his grave, although a world wept there"— it was true that his faith in God enabled him to teach in song what he learned in sorrow. His confession is significant, if it is tinged with sadness: "I have no friends. I must needs live alone, by myself, but I well know that God is nearer to me in my art than others. I converse with him without fear, evermore I have acknowledged and understood Him."

The biographer of Beethoven writes: "Beethoven was a being eminently chaste, and with deep Christian convictions. He could not conceive of love otherwise than according to the commandments of God. He expressed the sincerest aversion for such of his colleagues as boasted, after the manner of their time, of some adulterous relation . . . hence it is small wonder that his life furnishes no romantic liaison, no disorderly adventure, no criminal passion."

He was a lover of nature because he felt with Amiel that nature was seeking to express herself and he in turn was eager to hear her speak. He heard the voice of the Creator in the wind, and every natural beauty spoke to him of the presence and goodness of God. "When I am in the fields," he said, "I seem to hear every tree saying 'Holy! Holy! Holy!'"

For more than twelve years there lay on Beethoven's table a book by Sturm. He thumbed this book so much and so underscored his favorite passages that he had to procure for himself a second copy. In order that he might have it constantly before him, he copied from the book the following passage: "One might rightly denominate nature the school of the heart; she clearly shows us our duties towards God and our neighbours. . . . I would gain a knowledge of God, and through this knowledge I shall obtain a foretaste of celestial felicity." Few, perhaps, would find in nature such a means of blessing as Beethoven did, but that it lifted his whole soul nearer to God, there can be no question.

Beethoven died on March 26, 1827, during a great thunderstorm. None of his closest friends was with him at the end, but he was wonderfully sustained by the Christian hope of immortality. "The warring elements had been the composer's life-long friends, and often before had carried his soul above this little world. In the midst of the flashes and rumblings he said: 'I shall hear in heaven.' "

The French composer Charles Gounod will be remembered because of his immortal work, "Faust," which is sufficient in itself to give him a permanent place in the world's hall of fame. In 1839, at the age of twenty-one, he went to study at Rome, but before this he had already written a mass for the Church of St. Eustache so that, early in life, in spite of strong dramatic tendencies, he was attracted to sacred music.

Once at Rome he was deeply impressed with the decorative skill shown in the Biblical scenes in the Sistine Chapel. He wrote: "What a revelation in that tremendous creative gesture which gives the 'living soul' to the inanimate image of the first man, thus putting him in conscious relation with the principle of his being."

These sentiments reveal the source of his inspiration which enabled him to express the spiritual longings of "Faust" and other compositions such as: "Redemption" and "Mors et Vita," in which the religious exaltation is intense and sustained.

"In Gounod's two great oratorios, we have glimpses of his leanings toward a monastic life; his deep sense of the wonder and holiness of things unseen. Here and there, the 'representative themes'—an idea, no doubt, suggested by the growing vogue of Wagner—serve to guide the mind of the listener into certain trains of thought, the exquisite and mellifluous 'Redemption' *motif,* in particular, haunting the hearer's ear long after the sounds have ceased to be. A wonderful piece of writing—a gem of simplicity united to ethereal beauty—is the choral 'The Earth is My Possession.' In this we see more than one of the multiple phases of the composer's mind: his reverence for the Highest; his sense of the frailty of things human; his adoration of 'the Supreme offering of Supreme Love.' One feels that these great ground-themes are ever present with the musician throughout the course of his score, and they are tinged with a noble optimism—a belief in life triumphant after death—which reaches its culminating point in the 'Hymn of the Apostles' at the close of the Trilogy. In 'Mors et Vita,' the religious mysticism is, perhaps, deeper than in the 'Redemption,' nor does the latter work seem so suited to the concert-hall as for rendering within the solemn precincts of cathedral or church. The 'Redemption,' on the contrary, with its eminently singable chorus-work, its thrilling climaxes, and its wealth of melodic numbers as in 'From Thy love as a Father,' 'Lovely appear,' etc., has a certain luscious charm which, as was noticed in 'Faust,' links things human and divine." [6]

While many remember Felix Mendelssohn for his minor compositions, such as "Song Without Words," and "Spring Song," his greatest achievements were his religious oratorios, "Elijah" and "St. Paul." Few men, in any walk of life, have so exemplified the best qualities of religious character

---

[6] *Great Thoughts,* Volume 4, Series 6, page 266.

as did Mendelssohn. He was as gracious as he was gifted
and his death in 1847, at the early age of thirty-eight, caused
universal regret. A writer in the *Edinburgh Review* said:
"Rarely, if ever, has culture been more wisely and liberally
bestowed. . . . He was as gracious as he was gifted; evil
seemed to glance aside from him; temptation to get no hold
on him. He was singularly exact without pedantry. Everything that he acquired was ranged according to its value in
the chambers of a memory which nothing seemed to encum-
ber. . . . Though he was full of vivacity and humour, endowed with a keenness of observation not to be surpassed,
there was not a grain of mockery in his composition. He
delighted to admire and to venerate. In the practice of that
art which he exercised as naturally as other men exercise the
common gift of speech, in the regulation of his life, in his
public responsibilities, and in his domestic duties and affec-
tions, the whole career of Felix Mendelssohn bore the stamp
of a moral beauty of elevation not common among the sons
of men. Nothing vulgar, affected, or unclean could approach
him; no ungenerous thought ever touched him; he combined
the wit and readiness of a man of the world with the affectionate simplicity of boyhood. . . . He had a painter's eye
and a poet's heart. Everything that was good and beautiful
in Art or in Nature—no matter what the world, no matter
what the climate, no matter what the period—was not so
much seen and studied, as possessed by him. He was a
ready and exquisite linguist, endowed with that instinct for
subtlety in language of which many less perfectly educated
persons never dream. . . . He was a keen lover of literature.

. . . 'Complete' might have been the one word written on his tombstone, could it be applied to any human being." [7]

From the standpoint of popular appeal, the Italian composer, Giuseppe Verdi, must be ranked amongst the greatest of composers. It is over eighty years since the first performance of "Il Trovatore" and its popularity is greater than ever, and probably the same could be said of "Rigoletto." If Beethoven seemed to be visited with a succession of calamities, Verdi was so overwhelmed with misfortune that at one time he was in utter despair.

With advancing years his pessimism increased. The letters he wrote in answer to his friends on his seventieth birthday show with what melancholy his closing years were clouded. He was deeply moved by much that Shakespeare wrote and considered the creator of the morbid "Hamlet" "the greatest authority on the heart of man."

While endeavouring to complete an opera that had been promised, he was seized with a serious throat ailment which threatened his life. He no sooner recovered than his youngest child fell ill and soon afterwards died in the arms of its mother. Within a week his eldest daughter was taken ill and died. Overcome with sorrow at the loss of her children, Verdi's young wife fell an easy prey to brain fever and passed away two months after her children. In the midst of these terrible misfortunes, and with a soul torn with anguish, Verdi was compelled to finish the musical opera he had promised.

Like so many other great musicians, Verdi, in his later

[7] *Great Thoughts,* Volume X, page 280.

years, turned his attention to religious themes. He was all his life a devout Roman Catholic, and it is not surprising that he sought to enrich the music of his Church. His "Requiem Mass" is deeply impressive. It is a tribute to him that his pathetic triple blow, which threatened the wreck of his reason, if not his life, deepened his religious faith. He found inspiration in the Bible; its rich imagery was the source of many of his finest compositions. He wrote of the Bible: "That book, the reading of which has always been so dear to me." He spent the closing years in comparative retirement in a villa near Busseto, where his early life had been spent. The serenity which marked his closing years was in marked contrast to the agitation and unrest which has so often clouded the minds of great musicians. It can truly be said of him that, "He suffered and was strong." He died in 1901, at the advanced age of eighty-eight, loved by all.

There is just space left for a reference to another musician, this time a woman, not a composer but a vocalist, the Swedish nightingale, Jenny Lind. There have been many tributes to her genius and character, but one from Mendelssohn is significant. He wrote: "I have never in my life met so noble, so true and real an art nature as Jenny Lind. I have never found natural gifts, study, and sympathetic warmth in such a degree; and although one or the other quality may have appeared more prominently in this or in the other case, I do not believe that they have often been found united in such potency."

Born at Stockholm, Sweden, in 1820, Jenny Lind's remarkable gifts as a singer were soon discovered, and while yet a mere child she attracted not only the attention of musicians in her own country, but her fame spread to other lands. Whatever training did for her there can be no doubt that she was endowed with natural talents as very few have ever been. After a rehearsal, her teacher, Madam Erikson, said: "My child, I have nothing to teach you; do as nature tells you."

From childhood Jenny Lind was devoutly religious and this trait deepened during the passing years. "I sing to God," she exclaimed at the outset of her career, and from that high ideal she never turned aside. She was singularly free from vanity; "Connection with the stage has no attraction for me," she wrote to her old teacher, "my soul is yearning for rest from all these persistent compliments and this persistent adulation." Her private correspondence was invariably punctuated with many references to her Christian faith and reveals a hope which apparently was never dimmed. On learning of Mendelssohn's death in 1847, she wrote: "How glorious and strange are the ways of God! On the one hand, He gives all! On the other hand, He takes all away."

The Bible was her most precious book. She wrote to a friend: "My Bible was never more precious to me than now—never more truly my stay. I drink therein, rest, self-knowledge, hope, faith, love, carefulness, and the fear of God. Would that all men would come to this knowledge, and that we all daily feasted on this divine Book." The closing years of her life were spent in England, where she died in 1887.

CHAPTER SIX

Religious Faith of Great Philosophers

JOHANN WOLFGANG GOETHE, German poet and philosopher, has been called the Shakespeare of Germany. Matthew Arnold referred to him as the greatest poet of the present age and the greatest critic of all ages. Perhaps he was greater as a poet than as a philosopher yet increasingly with the passing of the years, he sought to understand the hidden meaning of life. Although at first prejudiced against Spinoza, he became enamored of the man and his philosophy and abandoning his earlier beliefs, he accepted the pantheistic position.

"Goethe entertained three fundamental views in common with Spinoza: the conceptions of the unity, the divinity, and the determination by necessity of the universe and all being. The unity and divinity of the world did not need to be proved to him; he felt them and saw them. The holy, inner, glowing life of nature revealed itself to him directly. He saw the inscrutable forces in the depths of the earth working together to create. The glorious formations of the infinite world moved all-living in his soul. When he saw the innumerable creatures, his brethren, passing by in the quiet bush, in the air, and in the water, he felt also the presence of the Almighty, the approach of the All-loving One, and he

94

then understood his soul as the mirror of the infinite God. Thus in himself he was assured of the unity of nature and God. In this respect he was also the perfect incarnation of the Storm-and-Stress movement, of which Spinoza naturally became the philosopher. He was justified in saying that it was his inborn way of viewing things, the very foundation of his whole existence, to see God in nature and nature in God." [1]

For a study of Goethe's philosophy and his views about religion we must turn to his masterpiece *Faust*. Here in one of the greatest poems ever written he represents the eternal significance of that conflict in human life between tendencies which degrade and plunge the soul into despair and the appeal of loftier things. It represents the utter folly of those who, betrayed by passion and desire like Esau, sacrifice the future for the present, who without reflection throw reason and conscience overboard and then suffer bitter disenchantment. Its sets forth with amazing dramatic appeal the utter inadequacy of this world to satisfy the soul's thirst for God.

In the second part of *Faust* there is the story of the soul's redemption but the deliverance wrought out is not in the Christian fashion for Goethe had broken away from the Christian conception of repentance and forgiveness. The potent influences in the soul's redemption or in the redemption of *Faust* were, first, the healing balm of nature; second, the service of the state; third, the influence of beauty; fourth,

---

[1] Albert Bielschowsky, *Life of Goethe,* p. 157.

the power of honest work and fifth, the service of humanity as an antidote to selfishness. His references to New Testament teaching are many. In fact his biographer points out that Goethe contended that no one had so completely interpreted the teaching of Jesus as had Spinoza. Here are some quotations showing his reflections upon life:

"I will listen to any one's convictions, but pray keep your doubts to yourself. I have plenty of my own."

"Let intellectual and spiritual culture progress, and the human mind expand as much as it will; beyond the grandeur and moral elevation of Christianity, as it shines in the gospels, the human mind will not advance."

"After all, what does it all come to? God did not retire to rest after the well-known six days of creation; but on the contrary, is constantly active as on the first. It would have been for Him a poor occupation to compose this heavy world out of simple elements, and to keep it rolling in the sunbeams from year to year, if He had not the plan of founding a nursery for a world of spirits upon this material basis. So He is now constantly active in higher natures to attract the lower ones."

"At the age of seventy-five one must, of course, think sometimes of death. But this thought never gives me the least uneasiness, for I am fully convinced that our spirit is a being of a nature quite indestructible, and that its activity continues from eternity to eternity. It is like the sun, which seems to set only to our earthly eyes, but which in reality never sets, but shines on unceasingly."

"To me the eternal existence of my soul is proved from

my idea of activity. If I work on incessantly to my death, nature is bound to give me another form of existence when the present one can no longer sustain my spirit."

"Thus convinced of a future for the aspiring and advancing spirit, Goethe faced the phantom which we call death. His last years were chastened by many sorrows, sorrows which all his wisdom and foresight could not evade, and for which his philosophy could furnish no anodyne, sorrows which might well have chastened into meekness the spirit of one aptly described by R. H. Hutton as 'the wisest man of modern days who ever lacked the wisdom of a child; the deepest who never knew what it was to kneel in the dust with bowed head and broken heart.' The most important achievement of his old age was the completion of the second part of *Faust*. He finished it before his last birthday, in his eighty-second year, and told Eckermann, his secretary, that, his task being done, he would regard the rest of his life as 'a pure gift.' In the following year he passed away, the last audible words from his lips as the shadow of death fell on him being 'More light! More light!' " [2]

That great man of letters, Dr. Samuel Johnson, in many respects one of the foremost English thinkers of his century, once wrote to his mother this letter which happily has been preserved: "Dear Honored Mother: Neither your condition nor your character make it fit for me to say much. You have been the best Mother, and, I believe, the best woman in the

---

[2] Robert P. Downes, *Hours with the Immortals*, p. 256.

world. I thank you for your indulgence to me, and beg forgiveness of all that I have done ill, and all that I have
omitted to do well. God grant you His Holy Spirit, and
receive you to everlasting happiness, for Jesus Christ's sake."

This was no spasmodic mood; Johnson was essentially a
religious man. "Indeed, it is no exaggeration to say that his
religion was the biggest thing about him. His face always
clouded when he recalled the fact that there was a time when
he paid no heed to such things. 'I was,' he once told Boswell, 'for some years totally regardless of religion. It had
dropped out of my mind. This was at an early part of my
life. Sickness brought it back, and I hope I have never lost
it since.' This memorable change took place in his university
days. 'When at Oxford,' he says, 'I took up William Law's
Serious Call, expecting to find it a dull book, and perhaps to
laugh at it. But I found Law quite an overmatch for me, and
this was the first occasion of my thinking in earnest about
religion after I became capable of rational enquiry.' From
that moment, he became a profoundly religious man. 'Indeed,' says A. C. Benson, 'I know no figure in biography
which illustrates more precisely and more convincingly, the
sort of religion of which the Englishman wholly approves.
There was not a touch of priggishness about Dr. Johnson;
he had no sort of sanctimoniousness; he said innumerably
severe, humorous, sensible, provocative things. He was full
of prejudices and fancies; but he was a wholly serious man,
and, what is more remarkable, a devoutly religious man. He
never suffered anything that was profane or sceptical, he disliked light-minded speculation on the mysteries of life and

death; he had the firmest faith in revealed religion and Christian doctrine."

In August, 1773, he visited Scotland and before going selected from Boswell's shelves, Ogden's *Sermons on Prayer,* which he read carefully as he travelled and discussed it with appreciative enthusiasm. When Boswell was about to leave England on a voyage to Holland—a much more hazardous undertaking than it would be now—they went and looked at Harwich Church. They entered the building and Boswell writes: "Having gone into it and walked up to the altar, Johnson, whose piety was constant and fervent, sent me to my knees, saying, 'Now that you are going to leave your native country, recommend yourself to the protection of your Creator and Redeemer.'"

In 1776, when he was sixty-seven, the great philosopher wrote in his private diary: "O God, who has ordained that whatever is to be desired is to be sought by labour to good effect, look with mercy upon my studies and endeavours. Grant me, O Lord, to design only what is lawful and right; and afford me calmness of mind and steadiness of purpose, that I may so do Thy will in this short life, as to obtain happiness in the world to come, for the sake of Jesus Christ our Lord."

Thomas Carlyle, although he broke away from creeds and churches, was at heart a Puritan. Sincere, sometimes brutally frank in his quest for reality, he had no patience for institutions which even suggested pretense or sham.

Perhaps his greatest contribution is that "he has helped to

uncrown the worthless and enshrine the noble in their place."
Leslie Stephen said of Carlyle: "The difference between
Carlyle and his Scottish forefathers was one rather of particular beliefs than of essential sentiment. He had changed
rather the data on which his convictions were based, than
the convictions themselves. He revered what his fathers
revered, but he revered the same principles in other manifestations, and to them this would appear naturally as a
profanation, whilst from his point of view it was but a legiti-
mate extension of their fundamental beliefs."

It is true that Carlyle was a man of moods and in some of
his iconoclastic burst of indignation said things that in calmer
temper he modified. Nothing, however, could be more gracious
and tender than this tribute to his mother in *Sartor Resartus*:
"My kind mother . . . did me one altogether invaluable
service: she taught me, less indeed by word than by act and
daily reverent look and habitude, her own simple version of
the Christian Faith."

"My mother, with a true woman's heart, and fine though
uncultivated sense, was in the strictest acceptation Religious.
How indestructibly the Good grows, and propagates itself,
even among the weedy entanglements of Evil! The highest
whom I knew on Earth I here saw bowed down, with awe
unspeakable, before a Higher in Heaven: such things, especially in infancy, reach inwards to the very core of your being;
mysteriously does a Holy of Holies build itself into visibility
in the mysterious deeps; and Reverence, the divinest in man,
springs forth undying from its mean envelopment of Fear."

His deep sympathy with all who suffered and his passionate love of Justice caused him to become impatient with the slow moving reforms of his day. Only a thoroughly sincere man could have had such lapses into pessimism and petulance as he knew, yet from such moods he did emerge to a faith that was ever militant and restless.

Nothing is so characteristic of Carlyle, and of his religious convictions, as his defence and interpretation of Cromwell's character. Carlyle's defence of Cromwell did much to reinstate the great Protector in the graces of the British people. Certainly in their attitude to the rights of kings, Carlyle and Cromwell were in complete accordance. But that which above everything else enabled Carlyle to interpret the life of Cromwell was his deep sympathy for the Puritan's religious faith, sympathy which was singularly lacking in many other critics. There were historians who saw nothing in Cromwell but the ravings of a fanatic or the subtle devices of a hypocrite. Carlyle's attitude was altogether different. When Cromwell writes of his conversion and delivery from sin, Carlyle understands exactly what he means. Furthermore, he knows to what Cromwell refers when he writes of his admission into the company of the redeemed. Carlyle snatched Cromwell from bitter and prejudiced detractors and it is safe to say "Put him on a pedestal from which he is not likely ever to be removed."

It would not be difficult to cull from the works of Carlyle sufficient passages to indicate a sceptical attitude towards religion, yet he was indignant when in 1853 Sir James Stephen charged him with unbelief. "You must have the goodness to expunge the phrase," he retorted. "I have merely said that no man ought to affirm what he does not himself completely believe. My own creed is not one of scepticism or doubt; but, for these thirty years, it has been *a certainty* with me, for which I am, and ought to be, for ever thankful to the Maker of me."

Of that thinker, John Ruskin, the critic, G. K. Chesterton, says: "As an artist in prose, Ruskin is one of the most miraculous products of the extremely poetical genius of England." This is no exaggerated estimate of Ruskin, for his marvellous versatility made him a great figure in several spheres. He was an authority in art, in industry, in economics, as well as in literature. He was an independent and courageous thinker. He was not a Christian of the conventional type any more than was Carlyle whose disciple he claimed to be. The two had much in common. Both hated the sham and superficial, and it would not be difficult to select passages from Ruskin's books in which he writes with biting sarcasm of much that was paraded as Christianity. Undoubtedly he renounced the evangelical views he held early in life but when it was rumoured that he was considering entering the Church of Rome he repudiated the report.

"I shall be entirely grateful to you if you will take the trouble to contradict any news gossip of this kind which may be disturbing the minds of any of my Scottish friends. I was, am, and can be, only a Christian Catholic in the wide and eternal sense. I have been that these five-and-twenty years at least. Heaven keep me from being less as I grow older! but I am not more likely to become a Roman Catholic than a Quaker, Evangelical, or Turk."

In his *Præterita,* he tells what he owed to the Bible, not only because of its literary beauty, but as a help and guide in creating his character. He writes: "My mother forced me by steady, daily toil to learn long chapters of the Bible by heart; to read it every syllable through aloud, hard names and all, from Genesis to the Apocalypse, about once a year. And to that discipline—patient, accurate, and resolute—I owe not only a knowledge of the Book, which I find serviceable, but much of my general power of taking pains, and the best part of my taste in literature."

As a potent factor in his life, Ruskin said of the Bible: "I have read that book, with as much care as most men, for forty years, and am thankful that, on those that trust it, I can press its pleadings. My endeavour has been uniformly to make men trust it more deeply than they do; trust it, not in their own favorite verses only, but in the sum of all; trust it, not as a fetish or talisman, which they are to be saved by daily repetition of, but as a Captain's orders to be heard and obeyed at their peril."

Ruskin wrote much about religion; nearly all his books abound in Scriptural quotations and his references to organized religion vary from petulant abuse to warm eulogy. His impatience and irritation with what he considered to be crude and ill-considered forms of religion did not lessen his deep reverence for spiritual things; he was essentially a believer.

"He had lived a long and varied life, giving his gifts lav-

ishly for the uplift of men, and especially that he might show
the toiler how to see life and see it whole. And when the
sun was setting, he wrote from the sweet solitude of Conis-
ton: 'I grow daily more sure that the peace of God rested
on the dutiful and kindly hearts of the laborious poor; and
the only constant form of pure religion was in useful work,
faithful love and stintless charity.' He had flung aside the
superficialities that satisfied so many. He stripped the hypo-
critical of their cloak, and pilloried abuses with which men
had long grown familiar. He saw that the true rationalism
was not in discarding this belief or that, but in turning religion to practical account, so that man's life might be redeemed from the curse of monotonous and meaningless toil,
and that in striving to do his best, he should 'adorn the doctrine of God our Saviour in all things.' Man had missed the
way pointed out by Christ and those who prepared the way
for Him. 'What doth the Lord require of thee but to do
justly, and to love mercy, and to walk humbly with thy God.'
And Ruskin's word to the modern world is: 'Do but learn so
much of God's truth as that comes to; know what He means
when He tells you to be just: and teach your sons that their
bravery is but a fool's boast, and their deeds but a firebrand's
tossing, unless they are indeed Just men, and Perfect in the
Fear of God; and you will soon have no more war, unless it
be indeed such as is willed by Him, of whom, though Prince
of Peace, it is also written, "In Righteousness He doth judge,
and make war." ' " [8]

---

[8] J. W. G. Ward, *Messages from Master Minds*, p. 242.

The somewhat whimsical Oliver Wendell Holmes was a man of strong religious faith. His father, a Congregational minister, cherished the hope that he would enter the ministry of the Church. But the stern attitude of many otherwise good people whom he met, and the hard doctrines he heard expounded as a boy, grated on his sensitive mind and he turned away from that calling. Yet he recognized the sincerity of those with whom he disagreed, and, in his own way, Holmes became a prophet, guiding many to God who might otherwise have lost their way.

Throughout the whole of his life, Holmes showed his revolt against the doctrines which, to him at least, seemed unattractive and unconvincing, but for the infinite tenderness and winsomeness of Jesus, he had nothing but reverence and obedience. In one of his delightful conversations with the Lady at the Breakfast Table, she propounded to him a question and the reply sets forth the position of Dr. Holmes himself. "Religion is not a matter of intellectual luxury to those of us who are interested in it, but something very different. It is our life, and more than our life, for that is measured by pulsebeats, but our religious consciousness partakes of the Infinite, towards which it is constantly yearning. It is very possible that a hundred or five hundred years from now the *forms* of religious belief may be so altered that we should hardly know them. But the sense of dependence upon Divine influence, and the need of communion with the unseen and eternal, will be then just what it is now. No geologist's hammer, or astronomer's telescope, or naturalist's microscope, will take away the need of the human soul for that Rock to rest upon which is higher than itself, that Star which never sets, that all-pervading Presence which gives life to all the least-moving atoms of the immeasurable universe." Speaking of the ministry of trouble in his own life, he gives what is unquestionably his own experience: "I am one of thousands who have had the same experience. They have been through the depths of human affliction, and know the needs of the soul. It will find its God in the unseen—Father, Saviour, Divine Spirit."

Another great American thinker, who, although finding himself at variance with contemporary religious leaders, had unfailing faith in Divine wisdom and power and goodness, was Ralph Waldo Emerson.

Emerson's theology was not satisfactory even to the Unitarian Church to which he belonged. His critics contended that he confounded Christianity with Pantheism and put the Bible on the same shelf as the Koran. In 1832 he resigned his pulpit, the immediate occasion for the step being his adoption of views in relation to the Lord's Supper which were in conflict with those held by his congregation. Yet his life was gracious and dignified. Father Taylor, a Boston evangelist said: "Mr. Emerson may be this or that but he is more like Jesus Christ than anyone I have ever known. I have seen him when his religion was tested and it bore the test." Matthew Arnold said of him: "He was the friend and aider of those who would live in the spirit." "He was the finest outcome of the most finely sifted English Puritanism transferred to a new soil, braced by generations of simple, healthy, pious life and saved from narrowness by a broad and genial culture. The gentle descendant of a noble succession of New England Puritan divines, living a pure and happy life in a dreamy country town, he was absolutely free from the domination of the dollar and devoted to a quest for truth unfettered by the idea that he could see the whole world from his own Church steeple. The fountains of his inner life were so deep and so secluded that they never became turbid or defiled by sense or outward things." [4] He believed that God was near. As Wordsworth recognized God in the beauties of nature, Emerson saw God in humanity. God, he taught, was not far removed from the world of men and things; he was in the human soul.

"A prominent feature in the teaching of Emerson is the immanence of God in Nature and in the human soul. The human soul stands in an intimate relation with the Universal Soul, the Eternal Spirit that men have named God. That Soul stands in living relation to our personality and it is our duty and our joy to cultivate that relation. The life of God overflows into our own if the channel be clear. Without this life we do not truly live. We may nourish 'a dull life within the brain,' but we do not partake of the true life, the life which is in its nature eternal. 'We lie open to the deeps of spiritual nature, to the attributes of God.' " [5]

Whatever objections may have been taken to Emerson's optimistic teaching, none would deny his deep reverence, transparent sincerity, and unswerving faith in God. He had

[4] *Great Thoughts*, Vol. 5, Series 7, p. 344.
[5] *Ibid.*, p. 345.

little patience, it would almost seem little understanding, of
unbelieving minds. To him faith in the goodness and wisdom of God came naturally. His own poem on the charm
and blessing of public worship is a tender testimony of his
regard for it:

"We love the venerable house
    Our fathers built to God—
In heaven are kept their faithful vows
    Their dust endears the sod.

"Here holy thoughts a light have shed
    From many a radiant face
And prayers of humble virtue made
    The perfume of this place.

"And anxious hearts have pondered here
    The mystery of life,
And prayed the eternal Light to clear
    Their doubts, and aid their strife;

"For faith and peace and mighty love
    That from the Godhead flow,
Showed them the life of Heaven above
    Springs from the life below."

The earliest works of the German philosopher, Rudolf
Christoph Eucken, dealt with the philosophy of Aristotle, but

his later works were mainly concerned with ethical and religious problems. He rejected naturalism and distrusted pure intellectualism. While regretting that historical religion often became contracted and impoverished, he insisted that it was man's duty and privilege to overcome his non-spiritual nature by incessant striving after spiritual life—a magnificent and worthy struggle which, called forth all his faculties including will and intuition.

"Eucken's attitude to dogmatic Christianity has found suggestive and sympathetic expression in 'Can we still be Christians?' In this volume he begins with a very lucid and penetrative discussion of the meaning and objective of Christianity, of those elements in the time-spirit which oppose and militate against the Christian view of God and the world, and of those elements in Christianity which would make its final rejection by our time a *felo de se*. The next section covers familiar ground in recapitulating the fundamental function of religion in realising the life of the spirit and its progress from universal to characteristic religion. In the final and constructive section he deals with the right of Christianity and its power to express itself in new forms, with the impossibility of effecting such a renewal within the Churches as they at present exist, and with the necessity of a new Christianity for our age. 'We have asked,' he says in closing, 'whether we of today can still be Christians. Our answer is not only that we can be, but that we must. But we can only be Christians if Christianity is recognised as a world-historical movement still in flux, if it is shaken out of its ecclesiastical vitrification and placed upon a broader basis. In this lies the task of our time and the hope of the future.' " [6]

In the Deem Lectures, which Eucken delivered in New York in 1913, he insisted that man was everywhere and always a moral being, even when his systems of morality often appeared to conflict with his own interests. But man's moral struggle, if pursued, inevitably leads to spirituality; this is the history, he insists, of all great earnest souls as St. Augustine and Martin Luther; "From inner conflicts was born the sure and triumphant conviction of a higher power in the movement towards morality—a power which not only imposes moral obligations on man, but which by the revelation of a new life gives him strength to fulfil them."

"It is the essence of all deep religions and especially of Christianity that a new life is created in man by a revelation of the Divine by means of a direct union of the soul with God. This new life is held to be superior to the complexity of existing conditions, and is sure to triumph because it is founded in God. A source of life is thus opened up which imparts new activity to a life hitherto stagnant. Man regains courage and confidence because he feels himself sustained by divine strength and love. No contradiction in the world of external realities is now able to weaken man's inner certitude. A powerful impulse towards work and creative activity will be born of the gladness within his soul. This explains the unquestioning confidence and joyous energy manifested by all the leaders of religious life; the consciousness of their deliv-

* E. Hermann, *Eucken and Bergson, Their Significance for Christian Thought*, p. 101.

erance from dire distress filled them with unbounded gratitude which sought expression in unremitting work for their fellow-men. Luther says: 'From faith flow love and joy in the Lord, and from love a free and joyous spirit of voluntary service for our neighbour quite irrespective of gratitude or ingratitude, praise or blame, gain or loss.' " [7]

"His attitude towards the person of Jesus is one of profound and reverent appreciation. In 'The Problem of Human Life' no less than a third of the whole volume is devoted to the great Teacher and Initiator of a new life. And nowhere does he join beauty to strength so harmoniously as in his word-picture of Jesus—a tribute in which the poet that is in every great thinker unites with the philosopher in a harmony of peculiar charm. Seldom has the perfect man and religious genius been limned with so persuasive a combination of strenuous thought and gracious word; we seek in vain either for the vapid sentiment of a merely romantic admiration, or for the desiccating touch of unemotional enquiry. Nor does he regard Jesus as a 'mere man,' to use a convenient phrase, but rather as a fontal personality. We not only see light in His light; we kindle our light at His. 'He who makes merely a normal man of Jesus,' he says, 'can never do justice to His greatness. Modern historical research protests against such a flat rationalisation, and insists upon a recognition of the undiluted reality.' In another passage he speaks of the unique position which Jesus occupied, not only in the believing hearts of His followers, but in His own consciousness." [8]

---

[7] Eucken, *Present Day Ethics*, p. 112.
[8] E. Hermann, *Eucken and Bergson, Their Significance for Christian Thought*, p. 103.

Sir Henry Jones, for many years Professor of Moral Philosophy in Glasgow University and one of the most distinguished philosophers of his generation, not long ago published his reflections on life under the title, *Old Memories*. "My Mother," he writes, "her father and her father's father, were very deeply religious. They were 'members' of their church, not simply 'hearers' or 'attendants.' The members were a select few, who stayed behind for more intimate spiritual communion when the mass of the congregation walked out at the end of the sermon." Sir Henry's account of his boyhood days makes delightful reading. The income in his father's home never averaged more than a few shillings a week. Only the bare necessities of life were obtainable, yet he never regretted the frugality and simplicity of that home. Likewise the little Sunday school and Welsh Calvinistic Methodist Chapel were potent and permanent influences in his life. He wrote: "I owe a great deal to a farmer named Robert Hughes. He took the Sunday school class in hand of which, with some four or five boys a little older than myself, I was a member, after all the other Sunday school teachers had refused to have anything to do with us—so endless was our mischief. He opened the Bible for the first time to me and to the other boys, and made us feel something of its qualities. The book of Job, owing to his dealing with it during my childhood, has been one of my first favourites ever after.

"I cannot pretend to measure the influence of the chapel and the traditions which were current amongst those who attended it upon my life and character. I think my religious beliefs are less crude now as well as shorter than they were in those days; but the essentials of the faith, the hypothesis on which I would fain say that my life rests, and without which the world would seem to me to be a wild chaos and the life of man a tragical blunder—*that* remains the same. We certainly wasted none of the opportunities that the chapel offered. As a matter of fact my mother sent John and me there, where we would be safe and out of the way. We were there practically every night of the week, except Saturdays, and our Sundays were especially crowded. I wonder if the Scottish Church can beat our record." [9]

His exalted position and prestige never prevented Sir Henry Jones from furthering the Kingdom of God whenever opportunity presented itself. When professor at Bangor College in Wales, he frequently took long journeys on Sundays that he might preach to scattered congregations of Calvinistic Methodists. The devotion of this great philosopher to the simple truths of the Christian religion is remembered by all who came into contact with him.

---

[9] Sir Henry Jones, *Old Memories,* pp. 58 and 59.

CHAPTER SEVEN

Religious Faith of Great Poets

FOR any study of Shakespeare, and especially if one is interested in the moral trend of his work, the age in which he lived should be remembered. There was a rude frankness, amounting almost to grossness, that was quite common. Furthermore, Shakespeare wrote for the theatre, a fact which accounts for many passages which otherwise might not have found a place in his works. Nevertheless, Shakespeare ranks as one of the greatest moral teachers of all time although such teaching is done indirectly, and while he did not have that sense of consecration to God which characterized John Milton, his faith in God is clear and emphatic.

He did not aim at teaching morality by precept, yet all his works indirectly teach the moral order of the world. He does not quote directly from the Bible, but he reveals an intimate knowledge of it, and in scores of striking passages one recognizes this fact. He holds, as it were, a mirror up to nature and shows how inevitably sin is punished; teaches in all his works that there are moral rewards and penalties. Over and over he demonstrates that:

> "The gods are just and of our pleasant vices
> Make instruments to plague us."

"Outward success and failure (in Shakespeare) are not the measure of the regard of heaven. The rewards and penalties of heaven are inward, and move within the region of the soul.

"If Macbeth, winning his heart's desire, were left with a tranquil and expanded heart; if in the outward triumph of his hopes he had the inward triumph of his spirit; then it would be reasonable to hold that heaven was indifferent and regardless.

"But the horror of the tragedy is this, that in accomplishing the evil he was set on, all that makes life beautiful departs from him, and he moves down into the darkness of the night.

" 'Be sure your sin will find you out,' says Scripture. It does not say your sin will be found out. It says that sooner or later it will find you out, in the deep and secret places of the soul. And the awfullest horror in 'Macbeth' is not the murder of the helpless Duncan; it is the way in which Macbeth's sin found him out.

"His soul shrank and shrivelled; all that was sensitive in him turned to stone; he became the prey of agonizing fears; he could not sleep—'Macbeth hath murdered sleep.' Suspicion haunted him; terror was round about him; life was a living death. He lost all kinship with what was fair and lovely; he 'made his bed in hell.'

"Remembering that, how can one believe that to Shakespeare heaven is morally indifferent? How can one say that God does nothing? Such judgments are entirely invalid unless one deliberately ignores the soul, and that is what Shake-speare never did." [1]

This tragedy of Macbeth presents, perhaps more forcibly than any other drama in all literature, the utter misery of a troubled conscience. To Shakespeare, evil was something which wrecked and ruined and destroyed. There was no escaping its dire consequences, and heaven was always on the side of the good. He taught that for a time goodness might seem to be vanquished and evil triumphant, but the terrible punishment following wrongdoing was inevitable, because it was in the very nature of the universe that wrong could not remain victorious.

There is evidence everywhere in his works that Shake-speare thought much on the deep problems of life, and his thinking led him to have faith in the wisdom and goodness of God even when His ways are mysterious. In "Anthony and Cleopatra" he makes one of his characters speak thus of un-answered prayer:

"We, ignorant of ourselves
    Beg often our own harms, which the wise powers
    Deny us for our good; so find we profit
    By losing of our prayer."

"Goodness may be vanquished, but our heart remains upon the side of goodness. Evil may be victorious, but we loathe it even in its victories. In the dark mysteries of many-coloured life, man at his deepest sides with what is good, and so doing aligns himself with God.

[1] George H. Morrison, *Christ in Shakespeare,* pp. 28 and 29.

"If Shakespeare left us sullen and despairing, we might flee for refuge to the gods of pessimism. But that is precisely how he never leaves us, though the stage be strewn with the bodies of the good. He leaves us with the glowing certainty that the good are the real victors though they perish, and that heaven, though dark with cloud, is on their side." [2]

There is both tragedy and comedy in Shakespeare's works but there is never flippancy where sacred things are concerned. His deep reverence is everywhere manifest. Every reference to holy things is marked by impressive reserve. Here is his reference to the Holy Land in "Henry IV":

"Those fields
Over whose acres walked those blessed feet
Which, fourteen hundred years ago, were nailed
For our advantage to the bitter cross."

John Milton differed from Shakespeare in many ways and especially in his presentation of religious truth. He expressed his own faith in clear terms. He wrote that he hoped to accomplish his work "by devout prayer to the Eternal Spirit which can enrich with all utterance and knowledge, and sends out His seraphim with the hallowed fire of His altar to touch and purify the life of whom He pleases." There was ever with Milton a deep sense of responsibility to God. He called men to courage and faith, nerved them to new endeavours and set them a magnificent example of fortitude under great suffering. He said:

---

[2] *Christ in Shakespeare,* pp. 38 and 39.

"I may assert Eternal Providence
And justify the ways of God to men."

After having read the devout vows and solemn promises
to God that Milton made, Dr. Samuel Johnson exclaimed:
"From promises like these, at once fervid, pious and rational,
we might well expect 'Paradise Lost.' "

Milton lived through troublous times. There was the bitter struggle between king and people. Following the execution of King Charles I, Milton was appointed Secretary of
Foreign Tongues, but after the Restoration his enemies became active and he needed all his faith in God to sustain his
courage and conviction. Whatever were the shortcomings
of the Puritans, even so impartial an historian as Macaulay
describes the moral corruption of the Restoration period:
"There came days, never to be recalled without a blush, the
days of servitude without loyalty, and sensuality without
love, of dwarfish talents and gigantic vices, the paradise of
cold hearts and narrow minds, the golden age of the coward,
the bigot, and the slave. The caresses of harlots and the
jests of buffoons regulated the policy of the State." Added
to this, his domestic affairs were far from happy and when
his eyesight failed him it seemed as though his cup of bitterness was filled to overflowing. Yet here his true greatness
revealed itself and he showed a spirit of submission to the
divine will which was sublime. Hope and Faith remained
strong in his soul and he refused to be crushed. He exclaimed:

> "These eyes, though clear,
> To outward view, to blemish or of spot,
> Bereft of light, their seeing have forgot;
> Nor to their idle orbs doth sight appear
> Of sun, or moon, or star, throughout the year,
> Or man, or woman. Yet I argue not
> Against Heaven's hand or will, nor bate a jot
> Of heart or hope, but still bear up and steer
> Right onward."

A biographer of Milton, Dr. Masson, says that he ever regarded religion as the chief concern in life. It was fitting that when he died his Bible should be lying open on the table beside his bed.

The poet Heinrich Heine may be said to have succeeded Goethe as the leading German poet. "Upon his shoulders," said Matthew Arnold, "incomparably the largest portion of Goethe's mantle fell." He was born of Jewish parentage at Dusseldorf in 1797. Later he abandoned Judaism and was baptized and received into the Lutheran Church at Heiligenstadt. Much of his poetry is exquisite; unequalled in German literature except possibly by the sonnets of Goethe.

In 1848 Heine suffered a stroke and for the remaining eight years of his life endured great pain with remarkable equanimity and even good humour. During these years of confinement to his room his mind grew clearer and more spiritual and he showed more sincerity than he did in his earlier works which, in many cases, were whimsical and satirical.

"The mysterious pains had greatly increased, and it had become evident that something more terrible than paralysis had taken possession of the enfeebled frame. But as the body died the mind more gloriously effloresced, like that fantastic flower of Borneo which displays its richest blooms as the stem rots slowly to the roots. New ideas, fresh impulses, creative instincts arose within him: his mental horizon widened, the atmosphere became more rarefied, the perspectives more alluring and more vast. . . . With bent body, half-blind, lame, without senses of smell or taste, with hands unable to guide the pen save for a few roughly-scrawled lines, with lips unable to respond to his wife's kisses, with ears painfully alert to any discordant sound, in straits of poverty, misunderstood, maligned, deceived, and defrauded, his was indeed a pitiable case. Had it not been for the sake of his wife and his old mother he would have put an end to his great misery, but he was of too heroic mould to entail suffering upon those who loved him by voluntarily plucking the dark fruit that grows so temptingly upon the boundary wall in the garden of life."

His enemies—and he had such strong antipathies himself that he was never without them—refused to believe in the genuineness of his conversion to Christianity. Certainly he was not of the orthodox type, nevertheless he had clear views and definite convictions about religion: "He hated priestcraft, whether Christian or Judaic, a paid clergy seemed to him a spiritual anomaly. But if clergy there must be, then let them be out-and-out exemplars of their faith; rather the fierce hell-threatening priest than 'the molly-coddle homœopathic soul-doctor who pours the thousandth part of a pint of reason into a gallon of morals, and sends people to sleep with it on Sundays.' And it is because he was a friend of Religion, and a friend of the Church, that he 'loathed that abortion called State-Religion, that monster born of the intrigue between temporal and spiritual power.' For notwithstanding all his repudiations and blasphemies Heine believed in a Supreme Power: *what* he knew not and does not try to explain. His sole *credo* is the very characteristic, 'I may not be over partial to anthropomorphism, but I believe in the Glory of God.' " [3]

Much has been written about the character of the Scottish poet, Robert Burns. In his fine essay on Burns, Robert Louis Stevenson says: "Burns was not devoted to religion, he was haunted by it." His way of living had done much to destroy that sense of joy and peace which his religious faith should have brought him. When a boy, Burns formed a friendship with a sailor-lad whose life at sea had made him wild and restless. Young Burns was drawn to him by what he thought was a fine spirit of chivalry and independence. Burns paid dearly for this companionship and, in commenting upon it later, wrote: "His friendship did me a mischief." Perhaps there is here a sidelight on those irregular habits which seriously affected Burns's life and work.

Burns lived in a time of religious controversy when disputants often became acrimonious and in this he shared with others. He wrote many poems in which he held his oppon-

---

[3] William Sharp, *Life of Heine,* pp. 205-206.

ents up to ridicule. A biographer wrote: "No one who reads
the satires the poet wrote on religious controversy of that
time can altogether acquit Burns of the bitterness of parti-
sanship, nor of a very daring and headlong rushing upon
matters of the most venerable and sacred character. Still,
remembering the times and circumstances, and pleading, as
we venture to do, that in him, amid all his aberrations, there
was a deep sense of personal religion, and an instinctive
admiration of all that was real and worthy in men and cus-
toms, we cannot shake off the conviction that, writing as he
did, he aimed not at injuring true morals or religion, but at
exposing and lashing sham and hypocrisy in human conduct, and superstition or abuse in religious observance. But,
in any case, in view of things as they then were and now are
in the matters dealt with, if it be asserted that Burns as-
sailed with ruthless hand and unsparing voice, it may be
justly replied that, to much good purpose, his was the hand
of a reformer and the voice of a prophet." [4]

On June 8, 1789, Burns wrote to his friend, Robert Ainslie,
the following letter:

"With respect to my welfare, a subject in which you once
warmly and effectively interested yourself—I am here in my
old way, holding my plough, marking the growth of my corn
or the health of my diary, and at times sauntering by the
delightful windings of the Nith—on the margin of which I
have built my humble domicile—praying for seasonable
weather, or holding an intrigue with the muses, the only

J. C. Higgins, *Life of Robert Burns,* p. 59.

gypsies with whom I have now any intercourse. As I am entered into the holy state of matrimony, I trust my face is turned completely Zionward; and, as it is a rule with all honest fellows to repeat no grievances, I hope that the little poetic licences of former days will, of course, fall under the oblivious influence of some good-natured statute of celestial prescription. In my family devotion—which, like a good Presbyterian, I occasionally give to my household folks—I am extremely fond of the psalm, 'Let not the errors of my youth,' etc., and that other, 'Lo, children are God's heritage,' etc., in which last Mrs. Burns—who by the bye, has a glorious 'wood-note wild' at either old song or psalmody—joins me with the pathos of Handel's 'Messiah.' "

"The Cotter's Saturday Night," with its deep reverence and tender regard for true religion, must ever be remembered as an expression of Burns at his best. There was much in the church of his day that was censorious and narrow, and there is some justification for his revolt which repeatedly finds voice in his poems. But none knew better than Burns himself how far he had strayed from what he himself called "early ingrained piety," which kept him innocent for many years. Burns was never happy in his sinning and there are passages in his poems which read like penitential psalms. There were times when penitence and aspiration flooded his soul. He had little patience with arrogant unbelief. He wrote:

> "An atheist's laugh's a poor exchange
> For deity offended."

Again he writes that to honor and revere God is natural and reasonable:

> "The great Creator to revere
> Must sure become the creature."

Perhaps the fullest and frankest expression of his views on religious matters is contained in the following statement taken from a letter written by the poet to Mrs. Dunlop:

"I have just heard Mr. Kirkpatrick preach a sermon. He is a man famous for his benevolence, and I revere him; but from such ideas of my Creator, good Lord, deliver me! Religion, my honoured friend, is surely a simple business, as it equally concerns the ignorant and the learned, the poor and the rich. That there is an incomprehensible Great Being, to whom I owe my existence, and that He must be intimately acquainted with the operations and progress of the internal machinery, and consequent outward deportment, of this creature which He has made—these are, I think, self-evident propositions. That there is a real and eternal distinction between virtue and vice, and consequently that I am an accountable creature; that from the seeming nature of the human mind, as well as from the evident imperfection—nay, positive injustice—in the administration of affairs, both in the natural and moral worlds, there must be a retributive scene of existence beyond the grave—must, I think, be allowed by every one who will give himself a moment's reflection. I will go further, and affirm that from the sublimity, excellence, and purity of His doctrine and precepts, unparalleled by all the aggregated wisdom and learning of many preceding ages, though, to *appearance,* He Himself was the obscurest and most illiterate of our species—therefore Jesus Christ was from God. Whatever mitigates the woes or increases the happiness of others, this is my criterion of goodness; and whatever injures society at large, or any individual in it, this is my measure of iniquity." [5]

This man, who in his soul believed in God, was more than "haunted by religion," and these words, written to his friend, Alexander Cunningham, point in that direction: "There are feelings and sentiments which, however the sceptic may deny them . . . connect us with, and link us to those awful obscure realities—an all-powerful and equally beneficent God, and a world to come, beyond death and the grave."

The English poet, William Wordsworth, nearly entered the ministry of the church. His religious views underwent some change yet his beliefs were never such as to prevent his taking clerical orders. His dissatisfaction with the state of society in England would have made his position as a clergyman of the Church of England extremely difficult.

Living in the beautiful Lake District of England, it is no wonder that the sensitive soul of this poet was so deeply moved with the beauty and charm of nature.

"He saw how Nature consecrated and made grand the human life which was lived among her beauty and sublimity.

---

[5] J. C. Higgins, *Life of Robert Burns,* p. 130.

Nature was conceived as a power inspiriting and ennobling man, and man as making Nature more sublime and fair. He turned from man as he is seen in cities, to man as he moved beneath the solemn hills and the watching stars. 'Love had he found in huts where poor men lie,' and he was the first poet in England who threw around the lives of ordinary men the glory and the sweetness of song. 'He was the first,' says Stopford Brooke, one of his finest interpreters, 'who poured around the dalesmen's cottages, and the wandering life of the pedlar, and the unheard struggles of the country and the mountain folk, the consecration and the poet's dream. He was the first who isolated life after life in tender and homely narrative, and made us feel that God was with simple men and women; that in their lives were profound lessons, that the same equal heart beat in the palace and the hamlet hidden in the hills; that all men were brothers in the charities which soothe and bless, in the moral duties which God demands, in the feelings which Nature awakens in their hearts; that a spirit of independence and stern liberty is the birthright and the passion of the poorest shepherd, as well as of the patriots who fill the pages of history.' " [6]

In *Messages From Master Minds,* Dr. J. W. G. Ward writes: "There is no mind more in tune with the infinite than that of William Wordsworth. He was the prophet of nature and his work is summed up in the phrase: 'Through nature to nature's God.' " Wordsworth never lost his way in his search for God. He could endorse, with all his heart and soul, that cry of Mrs. Browning:

---

[6] Robert P. Downes, *Hours with the Immortals,* pp. 107-108.

> "Earth's crammed with heaven,
> And every common bush afire with God."

This exactly expressed his view. Like Jacob of old, he would have exclaimed whenever he faced the beauty of nature, "Surely the Lord is in this place; and I knew it not!" To him, God was everywhere, as Dr. Ward writes: "Whether he moves through the silent places of the hills where he feels that his going is almost an intrusion, or by the quiet lakes that lie placid in the midst of the mountains, whether he lays his ear to the bosom of the earth that he may listen to the beatings of that mighty heart, or hearkens to the roaring winds that rush through the fastnesses of his native hills, it is the same God that is at hand:

> 'That being that is in the clouds and air,
> That is in the great leaves amongst the groves.' "

Wordsworth does not discuss vexed questions of faith so much as proceed on great assumptions. To him faith seemed the only right course to follow, it was the natural thing.

Temperamentally, he was not a doubter; he found it easy to believe that God—wise, just and merciful—was the Ruler of this world and in that calm, confident faith he lived and died. Writing to his friend, Sir George Beaumont, in 1825, Wordsworth said: "Theologians may puzzle their heads about dogmas as they will, the religion of gratitude cannot mislead us. Of that we are sure; and gratitude is the hand-maid to hope, and hope the harbinger of faith. I look abroad upon Nature, I think of the best part of our species, I lean upon my friends, and I meditate upon the Scriptures, especially the Gospel of John, and my creed rises up of itself, with the ease of an exhalation, yet a fabric of adamant."

Wordsworth's great contemporary, Alfred Tennyson, was the embodiment of culture that was rooted in religion.

"He was a man saturated through and through with faith in the invisible world which encompassed him, and of which he believed he had direct personal experience in those periods of trance or of mystic meditation which he described in his 'Ancient Sage,' and which he explained with more personal reference to his own experience to Professor Tyndall. Always it is with him, as he on one occasion exclaimed, 'What matters anything in this world without full faith in the immortality of the soul and of love?' Shakespeare and the Bible were his books of books. Jowett says: 'He spoke of two things, which he conceived to be beyond the intelligence of man, and it was certainly not repeated by him from any irreverence; the one, the intellectual genius of Shakespeare— the other the religious genius of Jesus Christ.'

"When asked as to his opinion about Christ, he would say, 'I have given my belief in "In Memoriam"'; but he used to say that the spiritual character of Christ was more wonderful than the greatest miracle. On another occasion he remarked, 'I am always amazed when I read the New Testament at the splendour of Christ's purity and holiness, and at His infinite pity.'

"Fully acquainted with all the difficulties of his age with

relation to Belief, an age which he himself described as a 'terrible age of unfaith,' he yet held bravely on to the truth which his soul had proved. We learn this from the inspiring lines:

"Cleave ever to the sunnier side of doubt,
  And cling to Faith beyond the forms of Faith!
  She reels not in the storm of warring words,
  She sees the best that glimmers through the worst,
  She feels the sun is hid but for the night,
  She spies the summer through the winter bud,
  She tastes the fruit before the blossom falls,
  She hears the lark within the songless egg,
  She finds the fountain where they wailed 'Mirage!' " [7]

His biographer writes: "He regarded the person and teaching of Christ with deepest reverence." Once, when he was walking in his garden, a friend asked him what he thought of Jesus. Tennyson made no answer for a while, then, pointing to a flower, he said: "What the sun is to that flower, Jesus Christ is to my soul." A. C. Benson, the critic, wrote: "That he regarded the Person and teaching of Christ with the deepest reverence is clear enough. He wrote, in 1839, to his future wife, that he was staying with 'an old friend' at Mablethorpe. 'He and his wife,' he writes, 'are two perfectly honest Methodists. When I came, I asked her after news, and she replied, "Why, Mr. Tennyson, there is only one piece of news that I know, that Christ died for *all*

---

[7] Robert Downes, *Hours with the Immortals*, pp. 277-278.

men," and I said to her: "That is old news, and good news, and new news;" wherewith the good woman seemed satisfied. I was half yesterday reading anecdotes of Methodist ministers, and liking to read them too . . . and of the teaching of Christ, that purest light of God.' . . . Tennyson said that Christianity, with its Divine morality, but without the central figure of Christ, the Son of Man, would become cold; and that it is fatal for religion to lose its warmth; that *The* Son of Man was the most tremendous title possible; that the forms of Christian religion would alter, but that the Spirit of Christ would grow from more to more 'in the roll of the ages'; that his line,

'Ring in the Christ that is to be,'

points to the time when Christianity without bigotry will triumph, when the controversies of creeds shall have vanished." [8]

It was the opinion of that distinguished literary critic, Clement Shorter, that Henry Wadsworth Longfellow was the best read poet for sixty years. His poems breathe, to an extraordinary degree, true Christian thought and feeling. He pleaded for the demands of love rather than for creedal statements of belief and he expresses, perhaps more closely than any other poet of the nineteenth century, the ideals of the vast majority of devout Christians. His sympathies were wide and deep and his faith in God was undimmed.

---

[8] A. C. Benson, *Tennyson,* pp. 110 and 111.

The tragic death of his first wife deeply affected him; the experience, however, enriched his spiritual life and enhanced his value as a poet: "To one who so soon knew the bitterness of farewell, there came the desire to know what lay behind the veil, so thin and filmy yet so opaque. He had lost the light of life. Was the lamp of faith to be extinguished by the chill winds of death? The writing reveals the writer, even as the penmanship may prove the identity of a man who signs a cheque. That all was not easy to bear at first, that there were some misgivings and fears, can be demonstrated when we look at the graphic story of Indian life, *Hiawatha*. When the warrior looks on the still form of Minnehaha:

> "His bursting heart within him
> Uttered such a cry of anguish,
> That the forest moaned and shuddered,
> That the very stars in heaven
> Shook and trembled with his anguish."

"The poignancy of parting is also glimpsed in another well-known poem, *The Reaper and the Flowers*:

> "There is a Reaper, whose name is Death,
> And, with his sickle keen,
> He reaps the bearded grain at a breath,
> And the flowers that grow between."

"But this is where hope cleaves the sombre shroud of sorrow, and looks on the face of the Reaper himself:

> " 'My Lord has need of these flowerets gay,'
>   My Reaper said, and smiled;
>   'Dear tokens of the earth are they,
>   Where he was once a child.'

> "Oh, not in cruelty, not in wrath,
>   The Reaper came that day;
>   'Twas an angel visited the green earth
>   And took the flowers away." [9]

The same poem bears witness to the triumph of Longfellow's faith. With what simplicity and insight he wrote:

> "There is no Death! What seems so is transition;
>   This life of mortal breath
>   Is but a suburb of the life elysian
>   Whose portal we call Death.

> "She is not dead—the child of our affection—
>   But gone unto that school
>   Where she no longer needs our poor protection,
>   And Christ Himself doth rule."

It is questionable whether any other poem in the whole realm of literature has been so much quoted as his "Psalm of Life." In his private life, Longfellow was singularly free from those faults that nullify the influence of so many men of genius, such as pride, jealousy and self-indulgence. His blameless life was a fitting accompaniment to his poetry.

---

[*] J. W. G. Ward, *Messages from Master Minds*, pp. 124 and 125.

A recent biographer of John Greenleaf Whittier en-deavours to dispel the popular conception of the Quaker poet as that of a "kindly, genial soul," and insists that he was decidedly militant wherever wrong was concerned: "Ostra-cised because of his abolition views, he portrayed men like himself, who were ready to sacrifice all comforts for the right deed or cause. He unconsciously incorporated in his work his own noble heroism. To the end of his days this militant Quaker admired heroes more than any other type of people. He was moved by any act of heroism, whether in the arena of politics or in the forum or in the field of battle, whether in private life or in the course of duty. His worship of the martyr type, which began in his boyhood, when he sang of heroic Quakers, almost became an obsession with him. He was thrilled and excited whenever he read about heroes and heroines." [10]

His passionate espousal of the Abolition Cause caused him to regard with distrust and indignation, clergymen who sup-ported the institution. At a pro-slavery meeting held at Charlestown, clergymen attended in a body. This caused him to thunder:

"Just God!—and these are they
Who minister at Thine altar, God of Right!
Men who their hands with prayer and blessing lay
On Israel's Ark of light. . . .

---

[10] Albert Mordell, *Quaker Militant, John Greenleaf Whittier*, p. 314.

"Paid hypocrites, who turn
Judgement aside, and rob the Holy Book
Of those high words of truth which search and burn
In warning and rebuke."

"His favorite doctrine was that of the goodness of God. He once said that the conviction of the loving fatherhood of God came to him after he had witnessed some kind act that his mother performed with tenderness for some erring person who had never anticipated such benevolence. He concluded that God always came to the rescue of the needy, even by human agency, but he failed to mention innumerable occasions on which the distressed clamoured in vain for aid. In the psychological terminology of today, a mother complex awoke in him the belief in the Eternal Goodness.

"Yet Whittier's doctrine of eternal goodness was needed in his time, to disintegrate the prevailing Calvinism with its emphasis on God's vindictiveness. It had a salutary influence upon the human mind, by liberating it from the effects of a baneful theological conception. He once told an English Quaker who visited him that he wrote his poem 'The Eternal Goodness' to counteract the Calvinistic teaching of God as tormentor. Yet, as he himself had a genuine conviction of sin, he was not very far removed from the tenets of Calvinistic theology.

"He thought that the natural corollary of his trust in a good God was a belief in the immortality of the soul. 'I do not think that God's love for His creatures ever ceases,' he said, 'or that probation closes with the grave. This view seems to me the necessary consequences of our retaining our personality in the after life. God will not in the resurrection make us mere automata. We must have the exercise of free will, the power of choice, or we cease to be ourselves.'

"Yet Whittier was not unaware of the compelling doubts that perplexed the believer. In 'Questions of Life,' written before Darwin had propounded his theory of evolution, Whittier presented the arguments of the sceptic with force and even conviction. He was familiar with the pantheistic conception of the universe, because of his studies in Oriental literature, and he had himself been in danger of yielding to its plausibility. Though he became intellectually entranced by it, he determined to reject it. He did not deny that he had his moments of uncertainty, though he never yielded to despair." [11]

In some respects Whittier had decided limitations. He was often harsh and even unjust with those who could not accept his views. He was disposed to speak of the "peculiar religious opinions" of those with whom he disagreed. Yet his integrity and sincerity were never questioned. He was more familiar with the Bible than any other American poet. He drew his inspiration from the Bible and the Quaker doctrine of the Inner Light. If he was sometimes baffled before some mystery, he accepted the situation as inevitable, but his faith remained undimmed. He believed that an answer would come to the soul's questionings; that in His own good time God would make all things plain:

[11] Albert Mordell, *Quaker Militant, John Greenleaf Whittier*, pp. 292, and 293.

"The same old baffling questions! O my friend,
I cannot answer them. In vain I send
My soul into the dark, where never burn
The lamps of science, nor the natural light
Of Reason's sun and stars! I cannot learn
Their great and solemn meanings, nor discern
The awful secrets of the eyes which turn
Evermore on us through the day and night. . . .

"I have no answer for myself or thee,
Save that I learned beside my mother's knee;
'All is of God that is, and is to be;
And God is good.' Let this suffice us still
Resting in childlike trust upon His will
Who moves to His great ends unthwarted by the ill."

When the poet Francis Thompson died in a London hospital on the morning of November 13, 1907, there passed
away one of the gentlest of men, and at the same time one
of the most erratic geniuses of modern times. His father
wished him to enter the priesthood of the Roman Catholic
Church and with that purpose in mind the boy was sent to
Ushaw College in the north of England. He showed no
inclination to study—except a few chosen subjects—and the
principal wrote to the boy's parents that, in his judgement,
their son was not fitted for the priesthood. At the close of
the letter he said: "I hope that God will enable you to bear
this disappointment. I quite agree with you that it is time
that Francis should prepare for some career. If he can

shake off a *natural indolence* which has always been an obstacle with him, he has ability to succeed in any vocation."

From that time until his death the story of his career is as strange as it is pathetic. After six years spent—mostly wasted—in a medical college at Manchester he went to London, where he lived for the remainder of his life. When he arrived there all he owned in the world were a few books and his meagre supply of clothing. It was the beginning of a bitter struggle against poverty and ill-health. He rarely wrote to his people.

In London he soon found his way to the Guildhall Library and other reading-rooms. He became more than ever careless about his appearance, and within a few months was almost in rags. Apart from taking opium, he was not a man of evil habits, indeed he was intensely religious, but he seemed utterly lacking in energy and ambition. Love of poetry had become a passion with him, and often he moved along London's crowded streets, seeing no one, his mind dwelling on some poetic subject.

He was soon spending his nights in common lodging-houses; occasionally he slept in arches or huddled on a bench by the Thames. If he had a few coppers he went to a lodging-house; if he had nothing, which was often the case, he slept on the Thames embankment. He saw much of wastrels and tramps and was quick to admire much in these outcasts of society. But vulgarity and obscenity of language or thought disgusted him and he saw much that made him heartsick. He established himself as a bootblack, but he was so harassed by the police ordering him to move on that he gave it up. He was glad to hold a horse's head for a few coppers. Sometimes he invested in matches that brought him a little interest on his money.

His fortunes began to change when in 1887, Wilfrid Meynell, editor of *Merrie England,* accepted a poem from Thompson for publication. From that time, until his death twenty years later, he was a constant contributor to magazines and the excellence and spiritual beauty of his poetry began to be recognized. It is not too much to say that he ranks as one of the greatest poets of modern times and that his religious poem, "The Hound of Heaven," is one of the enduring poems in our language.

This wonderful poem itself is probably his confession of faith. Indeed apart from his poetry it is difficult to state the religious beliefs of this extremely sensitive and timid genius. In spite of the wretched environment in which he lived so many years of his life, with the exception of the opium habit which he eventually shook off, Francis Thompson does not appear to have sunk into particular sins and as Wilfrid Meynell points out: "The argument of the poet's sanctity is in his poems."

At the time of his death he was engaged in writing *The Life of St. Ignatius.* His last ten days he spent in the Hospital of St. John and St. Elizabeth. He was deeply grateful to those who ministered to him and gladly received the Sacrament a few hours before he passed away.

CHAPTER EIGHT

Religious Faith of Great Scientists

THE English naturalist, Charles Robert Darwin, worked a revolution in biological science. He is often referred to as the one who discovered the doctrine of evolution. This has been vigorously denied even by many who are sympathetic toward his viewpoint. Matthew Arnold said, "I cannot understand why you scientific people make such a fuss about Darwin. It is all in Lucretius." To this Professor Judd remarked, "Yes. Lucretius guessed what Darwin proved." [1]

The central idea of Darwin's theory is that all forms of organic life are derived from a small number of primitive types, and all vegetable and animal organisms now existing, or having existed, owe origin to a slow operation of modifying influence of local or special causes transmitted hereditarily. These views he first advocated in his famous *Origin of Species* published in 1859.

Darwin published this epoch-making book after having, at infinite pains and by repeated tests and experiences, verified every conclusion he advanced. He admitted that much was obscure and would probably remain so, but the following

---

[1] S. Parkes Cadman, *Charles Darwin and Other Thinkers*, p. 12.

statement of his viewpoint indicates the sincerity of his conviction:

"I can entertain no doubt, after the most deliberate and dispassionate judgement of which I am capable, that the view which most naturalists until recently entertained, and which I formerly entertained—namely, that each species has been independently created—is erroneous. I am fully convinced that species are not immutable; but that those belonging to what are called the same genera are lineal descendants of some other and generally extinct species, in the same manner as the acknowledged varieties of any one species are the descendants of that species. Furthermore I am convinced that natural selection has been the most important, but not the exclusive, means of modification." [2]

The publication of Darwin's views aroused a controversy which unfortunately was marked by much bitterness. It came at a time when anything savoring of liberalism was strongly denounced, and by many leading churchmen his position was treated with ridicule and often with misrepresentation. Yet Darwin had had a thoroughly religious up-bringing. As a young man his frequent quotations from the Bible amused and sometimes irritated his friends. He had graduated from Cambridge University with the thought of becoming a clergyman. While he changed his position regarding many even of the fundamentals of religion, he was always devout, as he was sincere. His testimony to the reality of the Christian life is quoted in the life of James Chalmers. These words

---

[2] Introduction of *Origin of Species*, p. 6.

in themselves are a magnificent tribute to missionary work. Here is Darwin's own statement:

"Before we laid ourselves down to sleep the elder Tahitian fell on his knees, and with closed eyes repeated a long prayer in his native tongue. He prayed as a Christian should do, with fitting reverence and without the fear of ridicule or any ostentation of piety. At our meals, neither of the men would taste food without saying beforehand a short grace. Those travellers who think that a Tahitian prays only when the eyes of the missionary are fixed upon him, should have slept with us that night on the mountain side."

Some years later when standing amid the solitary grandeur of a Brazilian forest he felt the onrush of such feelings of wonder—almost of worship—that he wrote:

"The grandest scenes would not cause any such conviction to arise in me. It may be truly said that I am like a man who has become colour blind, and the universal belief by men in the existence of redness makes my loss of perception of not the least value as evidence."

With the passing of the years Darwin gave himself more and more to the study of physical science. In matters of religion he became an agnostic. He did not deny the existence of God. Furthermore he never lost his deep interest in such subjects as the soul, immortality and Providence.

In *The Evolution of Charles Darwin* (page 271) Dr. George A. Dorsey has this to say: "Darwin by intuition seemed to recognize insuperable difficulties (in matters of religion), and to have the good sense to follow the adage of his day: he looked them squarely in the face, and passed on.

He dwelt with concrete life as he found it. He left questions of Creators, Causes and Designs to theologians and metaphysicians. Darwin was a scientist, but he was no atheist."

The following words used by Darwin at the close of his *Origin of Species* could never have been written by an atheist:

"When I view all beings not as special creations, but as the lineal descendants of some few beings which lived long before the first bed of the Cambrian system was deposited, they seem to me to become ennobled. . . . There is grandeur in this view of life, with its several powers, having been originally breathed by the Creator into a few forms or into one; and that, whilst this planet has gone cycling on according to the fixed law of gravity, from so simple a beginning endless forms most beautiful and most wonderful have been, and are being evolved."

Thomas Henry Huxley, scientist, was a close friend of Darwin. He was born sixteen years after Darwin, but a friendship sprang up between them, and in the acrimonious discussions which followed the publication of Darwin's *Origin of Species,* Darwin found in Huxley a close ally and able advocate. He was if anything more interested in the moral and religious implications of Darwin's theory than Darwin himself. He believed that the whole controversy was due to misunderstanding and misrepresentation. He fought, with equal vigour, confused theologians on one hand and scientific dogmatists on the other. He held that the Holy Scriptures, if stripped of crude interpretations and century-old accretions, would be found to harmonize with Darwin's theory. He never ceased to hold the Bible in high esteem, and chose a religious education for his children. Here are his own words:

"Take the Bible as a whole, make the severest deductions which fair criticism can dictate, . . . and there still remains in this old literature a vast residuum of moral beauty and grandeur. . . . For three centuries this book has been woven into the life of all that is best and noblest in English history. . . . By the study of what other book could children be so much humanized and made to feel that each figure in that vast historical procession files, like themselves, between two eternities, and earns the blessings or the curses of all time, according to its effort to do good and hate evil, even as they also are earning their payment for their work." [3]

Yet Huxley steadily veered to agnosticism. He looked towards Christianity wistfully, but he had few positive and affirmative sympathies with spiritual realities. A belief in a personal Deity, especially one who controlled the destiny of the world and of man, was a faith he found it exceedingly difficult to accept. He wrote seven thousand pages so that his position is in no sense obscure. It would be possible to cull from these pages sufficient sympathetic references to religion to make him appear a believer, but such a course would not be fair as about his agnosticism there can be no question. He refused, however, to allow himself to be called either an atheist or a materialist. He remained during the greater part of his life a "reverent agnostic."

---

[3] Ainsworth Davis, *T. H. Huxley* ("English Men of Service," Series), p. 103.

In a letter written to Charles Kingsley in 1863, Huxley had said: "I have a great respect for all the old bottles, and if the new wine can be got into them and not burst them, I shall be very glad. I confess I do not see my way to it: on the contrary the longer I live and the more I learn the more hopeless to my mind becomes the contradiction between the theory of the universe as understood and expounded by Jewish and Christian theologians and the theory of the universe which is every day and every year growing out of the application of scientific methods to its phenomena."

At the close of another letter written to Kingsley soon afterwards he said: "I have never had the least sympathy with the *a priori* reasons against orthodoxy, and I have by nature and disposition the greatest possible antipathy to all the atheists and the infidel school." As late as 1892, in a letter to the *London Times* he insisted that evolution was not necessarily incompatible with theism.

He died on June 29, 1895. His gravestone bears three significant lines written by his wife—sentiments which we feel sure he would have heartily endorsed:

> "Be not afraid, ye waiting hearts that weep;
> For still He giveth His belovèd sleep;
> And if an endless sleep He wills, so best."

Alfred Russel Wallace has been called the co-discoverer with Darwin of evolution. This fact contained within itself the possibilities of jealousy and bitter acrimony, yet there was such consideration and mutual forbearance between the two men that their friendship is one of the most beautiful in the annals of scientific discovery. The conduct of both men is a lasting tribute to their sincerity and nobility. They were not identical in their points of view in that Wallace, in his explanation of the origin of man, introduces other important factors into the process. He does not deny the development of man's moral and intellectual faculties from animals, but he does affirm that these faculties have not evolved by a natural selection. He insists their operating cause cannot be discovered in the realm of natural law, but are to be found in the unseen kingdom of spirit. There were other points of departure, but this was the principal difference between the attitudes of the two men. Wallace was a Theist and throughout life remained so. He insisted upon the necessity of a Controlling Mind. In a letter written to Sir James Marchant he said:

"The completely materialistic mind of my youth and early manhood has been slowly moulded into the socialistic, spiritualistic and theistic mind I now exhibit—a mind which is, as my scientific friends think, so weak and credulous in its declining years as to believe that fruits and flowers, domestic animals, glorious birds and insects, wool, cotton, sugar and rubber, metals and gems, were all foreseen and fore-ordained for the education and enjoyment of man." [4]

As late as May, 1913, in another statement to the same writer regarding his religious beliefs, Wallace said:

"Recent discoveries demonstrate the need of co-ordinating

---

[4] From letter to Sir James Marchant, quoted in *The Revolt of Democracy*, p. 34.

power even in the very nature and origin of matter; and
something far more than this in the origin and development
of mind. The whole cumulative argument of my 'World of
Life' is that, in its every detail it calls for the agency of a
mind or minds so enormously above and beyond any human
minds, as to compel us to look upon it, or them, as a God or
Gods, and so-called 'Laws of Nature' as the action by will-
power or otherwise of such superhuman or infinite beings.
'Laws of Nature' apart from the existence and agency of
some such Being or Beings, are mere words, that explain
nothing—are, in fact, unthinkable.   That is my position!
Whether this 'unknown reality' is a single being, and acts
everywhere in the universe as direct creator, organizer and
director of every minutest emotion in the whole of our universe, and of all possible universes, or whether it acts through
variously conditioned modes, as H. Spencer suggested, or
through 'infinite grades of beings' as I suggest, comes to
much the same thing. Mine seems a more clear and intelligible
supposition as stated in the last paragraph of my 'World of
Life' and it is the teaching of the Bible, of Swedenborg and
of Milton!"

   Sir James Young Simpson, Scottish obstetrician, is chiefly
known because of his discovery of chloroform as an anæs-
thetic.   He was the first Scottish physician to receive a
baronetcy.   He made further notable achievements in gynecol-
ogy in which he was far in advance of his time. His prestige
in the medical profession ranks him with Harvey, Jenner and
Lister. His biographer, H. Laing Gordon, wrote, "He was

stimulated by a genius which gave him the energy to fight for his ends with Herculean strength. If we are asked what we most honour in Simpson we answer, 'Not so much the discoveries he made, the instruments he invented, nor the exposure of numerous evils, nor any particular contributions to science, literature or archæology, but rather for the inspiring life of the man.' He was guided by high ideals and a joyous unhesitating belief that all good things were possible— that right must prevail."

When he was asked what he regarded as the greatest discovery he had ever made, Sir James Young Simpson replied unhesitatingly, "That I have a Saviour." He was a man of singularly beautiful character, and accepted with heart and soul the Christian faith. With advancing years there came to him in matters of religion even clearer light, deeper peace and fuller conviction. During the thirty-eight years he carried on as a doctor he was never off duty, and his interest in religion was genuine. He accepted the evangelical point of view. He said, "I have unshaken confidence in Jesus only."

Lord Kelvin (William Thomson) was Professor of Natural Philosophy at Glasgow for fifty-three years. He had distinguished achievements to his credit in all domains of Dynamics, Sound, Light, Heat, Magnetism and Electricity. He was largely responsible for the success of the Atlantic cable laid in 1857. In some respects he might be called the first electrical engineer. He was president of the Royal Society in 1890-95. In his presidential address to the British Association in Edinburgh, Lord Kelvin said:

"I feel profoundly convinced that the argument from design has been greatly too much lost sight of in recent zoological speculations. But over-powering strong proofs of intelligent and benevolent design lie all around us, and if ever perplexities, whether metaphysic or scientific, turn us away from them for a time, they come back upon us with irresistible force, showing us through Nature the influence of a free-will, and teaching us that all living beings depend on one ever-acting Creator and Ruler."

In another connection when discussing the argument from design, Lord Kelvin wrote:

"Is it conceivable that the luminiferous ether should throw out these effects by chance—that the colours of the butterfly or of a beautiful flower should result from a fortuitous concourse of atoms, and that they should give pleasure to another fortuitous concourse of atoms constituting myself? The atheistic idea is so nonsensical that I do not know how I can even put the position into words." [5]

The work of the French chemist, Louis Pasteur, is widely known. He was the founder of the science of bacteriology. Due to his work we have pasteurization of wines and milk, to prevent deterioration and protect health. He was mainly responsible for the prosperity of the French silk trade by successfully combating the silkworm disease. His later years were devoted to the direction of the Pasteur Institute, built by popular subscription for the prosecution of research in the preventive treatment of infection. Perhaps he is best-known

---

[5] Victoria Institute, *Journal*, No. 124, p. 267.

because of his work in preventive medicine and his discovery of a cure for hydrophobia. Undoubtedly he was one of the greatest men of his generation. In religion he was a devout Roman Catholic. His own creed was beautifully expressed in his eulogy upon *Littré*: "He who proclaims the existence of the Infinite, and none can avoid it—accumulates in that affirmation more of the supernatural than is to be found in all the miracles of all the religions; for the notion of the Infinite presents that double character that it forces itself upon us and yet is incomprehensible. When this notion seizes upon our understanding, we can but kneel. . . . I see everywhere the inevitable expression of the Infinite in the world; through it, the supernatural is at the bottom of every heart. The idea of God is a form of the idea of the Infinite. As long as the mystery of the Infinite weighs on human thought, temples will be erected for the worship of the Infinite, whether God is called Brahma, Allah, Jehovah, or Jesus; and on the pavement of those temples, men will be seen kneeling, prostrated, annihilated in the thought of the Infinite." [6]

When delivering the funeral oration at the death of another great scientist, Henri Sainte Claire Deville, Pasteur said: "Oh! I implore thee, do not now look down upon thy weeping wife and afflicted sons: thou wouldst regret this life too much! Wait for them rather in those divine regions of knowledge and full light, where thou knowest all now, where thou canst understand the Infinite itself, that terrible and bewildering notion, closed for ever to man in this world, and

---

[6] René Vallery-Radot, *The Life of Pasteur*, p. 15 of the introduction.

yet the eternal source of all Grandeur, of all Justice and all Liberty." [7]

René Vallery-Radot says of this thoroughly religious man: "Pasteur soared without an effort into the domain of spiritual things. Absolute faith in God and in Eternity and a conviction that the power for good given to us in this world will be continued beyond it, were feelings which pervaded his whole life; the virtues of the Gospel had ever been present to him. Full of respect for the form of religion which had been that of his forefathers, he came to it simply and naturally for spiritual help in these last weeks of his life." [8]

The famous German-American electrician, Charles Proteus Steinmetz, came to America in 1889 when he was twenty-four years of age. He was almost refused admission by the United States immigration authorities. In some respects he was a sorry-looking spectacle, dwarfed and misshapen in body with defective eyesight and clothes decidedly shabby. Furthermore he could scarcely speak a word of English. After his admission to the country, however, he secured work with the General Electric Company at two dollars a day, and so proved his worth that he was given the position of chief-consulting engineer. He soon became one of the greatest authorities in the world on electrical engineering and mathematics: he was equally interested in pure and applied science. He wrote on the technical side of electrical engineering with

---

[7] *Ibid.*, p. 327.
[8] *Ibid.*, p. 462.

clearness and charm. Before he died in his sixtieth year many great distinctions came to Steinmetz, and his authority in his own field was virtually undisputed.

Steinmetz had deep religious convictions which were clear and emphatic. In an article contributed to *Harper's Magazine* in February, 1922, he said: "In the present state of human knowledge science can get no definite and final conclusions on these (religious) subjects, due to the limitations inherent in science. Science does not and cannot show the world as it actually is with its true facts and laws, but only as it appears to us within the inherent limitations of the human mind. The greatest limitation is that our observations are finite, and our intellects cannot grasp the conception of infinity. The same limitation, therefore, applies to the world as applies to our reasoning intellects, and in the world of science there is no infinite, and conceptions such as God, the immortality of the ego, etc., etc., are beyond the realm of empirical science. . . . Science deals only with finite events in finite time and space, and the farther we pass onward in space and time the more uncertain becomes scientific reasoning until in trying to approach the infinite we are lost in the fog of unreasonable contradiction, beyond science—that is transcendental."

Some time later Roger W. Babson when interviewing Mr. Steinmetz asked him this question, "What line of research will see the greatest development during the next fifty years?" After careful thought Steinmetz made this reply:

"I think the greatest discovery will be made along spiritual lines. Here is a force which history clearly teaches has been the greatest power in the development of men and history. Some day people will learn that material things do not bring happiness, and are of little use in making men and women creative and powerful. Then the scientists of the world will turn their laboratories over to the study of God and prayer and the spiritual forces which as yet have hardly been guessed at. When that day comes the world will see more advancement in one generation than it has seen in the past four." [9]

Jean Louis Agassiz, Swiss-American naturalist, was one of the ablest biologists of his day, and, in some respects at least, the most successful teacher of science that America has known. His main work was the study of fish forms and his research wrought revolution in the study of natural history. His principle like that of Fabre was to learn by actual first-hand contact with nature. He was the moving spirit in the foundation of the wonderful Harvard Museum of Comparative Zoology. He was singularly modest, a real friend and comrade to all the students. At the time of his death it was said of him: "He was a student all his life, and when he died he was younger than any of them."

He was unsympathetic to Darwinism due, in some part, to a misunderstanding as to the true meaning of those theories. He had an intensely religious mind, although he was totally out of sympathy with sectarianism and creedal statements. He had great independence of thought and warned his students

---

[9] Editorial in *The Christian Science Monitor.*

equally against religious traditionalists and dogmatic scientists.

He saw in every natural object "a thought of God." It was his custom when commencing a lecture to ask his pupils to join with him in a short silent prayer for God's companionship, and every one felt the depth of his sincerity, and his intense religious convictions. He disliked irreverence and flippancy when scientific matters were being discussed, and frequently showed impatience with materialists from whose point of view he was far removed. His attitude is well summed up in the following words delivered to his students at Penikese School: "I feel even more vexed at impropriety in a scientific library than in a church. The study of nature is intercourse with the Highest Mind. You should never trifle with nature. At the lowest her works are the works of the Highest Powers, the Highest Something in the universe in whatever way we look at it." [10]

Sir Oliver Lodge was born in Staffordshire, England, in 1851. When thirty years of age he was appointed Professor of Physics at University College, Liverpool. For more than half a century he was a close investigator of cosmic phenomena. During that long period there were few positions of scientific distinction that he did not occupy. He was President of the British Association and in 1919 was awarded the Albert Medal of the Royal Society of Arts for his work as a pioneer in wireless telegraphy. Sir Oliver Lodge was the author of many books and has repeatedly written with

---

[10] *The Scientific Monthly*, November, 1923.

frankness on religious matters.   Nothing would be clearer
than the following statement he made:

"I believe in one infinite, eternal being, a guiding, loving
Father in whom all things consist.   I believe the divine nature
is especially revealed to man in Jesus Christ, who lived, taught
and suffered in Palestine nineteen hundred years ago, and
has since been worshipped by the Christian Church as the
immortal Son of God and Saviour of the world.   I believe
the Holy Spirit is ever ready to help us along the way to
goodness and truth, that prayer is the means of the communion of man and God, and it is our privilege by faithful
service to enter life eternal, the communion of saints, and
the peace of God."

In 1910 Sir Olive Lodge published *Reason and Belief* in
which he clearly set forth his views in the following words:

"Modern science knows nothing of ultimate origins.   It
never asks the question.   It starts with matter in motion; it
traces its past, and to some extent its future.   It may look
backward and forward for millions of years; but to every
past, however ancient, there is an antecedent past; and nothing points to a beginning nor to an end.   At every point we
can ask: And what before? or, What after?   But a beginning
for this terrestrial globe, the earth, can be imagined: and at
a time when the earth and the universe were practically identical, the beginning of the earth would seem like the beginning
of all things.   And so a poetic account of the Creation is
handed down.   It is a representation of certain truths—that
there was gradual development of life on the earth—lower

forms first, higher later; that everything depended on the energising and brooding power of a pre-existent and eternal Divine Spirit; that matter is amenable to thought, design, conception; that everything is controlled by a purpose; that things in themselves, and save as marred by men, are on the whole 'good.'

"But then you will say that having accounted for the origin of everything, including a complete human race, a second legend begins, about the infusing of the Divine Spirit into Adam, and the fall. Yes, quite true. On a different level, and with a different purpose, this second, the so-called Prophetic narrative, has a notable meaning of its own; and we may be grateful to the ancient compilers of Scripture that they preserved both these beautiful documents, and left it for us to understand, and as far as necessary to harmonise them. Both have a truth of their own, both are inspired, and only to a shallow Sciolism are they inconsistent. Neither by itself is complete—they supplement each other—and certainly neither is to be taken as a statement of cold-blooded scientific fact. Science did not exist in those days. Science as we understand it is a modern growth. Through Science we learn of the Rise of man—a most hopeful doctrine. In Genesis is depicted a Fall—the beginning of a consciousness of free will, the entrance of sin. The two are by no means inconsistent; a fall often follows a rise—sometimes as a natural consequence. It is not difficult to interpret the legend of 'Adam.' A knowledge of good and evil, a recognition of responsibility—perception of a power of choice—must have dawned upon some early genius of the race, into whom entered the Divine breath of inspiration; that was the period when 'man became a living soul.' " [11]

For seven years before his death Sir Oliver Lodge became widely known because of his advocacy of personal survival after death through his investigations in the realm of psychical research. Three of his books on this theme aroused wide-spread interest. These were *Raymond or Life and Death; Science and Immortality,* and *Why I Believe in Personal Immortality.* He became thoroughly convinced that the case for survival after death could be attested by facts as convincing and logical as those generally accepted in other fields. He concluded a carefully written article entitled *The Scientific Argument for Personal Survival* with the following words:

"In this vital matter we are not left to inspirations and intuitions. Cold-blooded direct evidence is vouched for, and this it is which must be examined without prejudice either way. And this it is which will ultimately convince all humanity of the truth of survival, and incidentally will in the long run enable us to realise more clearly what survival means, what physical mechanism is associated with it, what is its scope and how far it extends, and what bearing it has on the ultimate problems of reality." [12]

The distinguished physician, Sir William Osler, was born in Ontario in 1849. After attendance at colleges in Toronto

---

[11] *Reason and Belief,* pp. 117-121.
[12] *Has Science Discovered God?* (a symposium by Edward H. Cotton), p. 266.

and Montreal, he was appointed Professor of the Institute of Medicine at McGill University, Montreal, in 1874. Ten years later he accepted a position in the University of Pennsylvania, and in 1888 he became head of the Department of Medicine in Johns Hopkins University at Baltimore. Later he became Regius Professor of Medicine at Oxford. It is not too much to say that for thirty years Dr. Osler was regarded as one of the foremost physicians in the world. Thousands of students had occasion to know that the literary charm of his lectures was equal in value to the remarkable, sane admonitions he gave to these young medicos. His lectures to doctors and nurses in part, at least, were published in a book *Counsels and Ideals*. These lectures reveal the extraordinary literary ability of Osler and his amazing aptitude in quoting the Bible in an effective manner. He was not dogmatic on religious subjects, but he had certain definite convictions as the following paragraph reveals:

"Begin the day with Christ and His prayer—you need no other. Creedless, with it you have religion; creed-stuffed, it will leaven any theological dough in which you stick. As the soul is dyed by the thought, let no day pass without contact with the best literature of the world. Learn to know your Bible, though not perhaps as your fathers did. In forming character and in shaping conduct, its touch has still its ancient power." [18]

His views on immortality are set forth in this excerpt from a lecture:

[18] *Counsels and Ideals*, p. 279.

"Though his philosophy finds nothing to support it, at least from the standpoint of Terence, the scientific student should be ready to acknowledge the value of a belief in an hereafter as an asset in human life. In the presence of so many mysteries which have been unveiled, in the presence of so many yet unsolved, he cannot be dogmatic and deny the possibility of a future state; and however distressing such a negative attitude of mind to the Teresian, like Pyrrho, he will ask to be left, reserving his judgement, but still enquiring. He will recognize that amid the turbid ebb and flow of human misery, a belief in the resurrection of the dead and the life of the world to come is the rock of safety to which many of the noblest of his fellows have clung; he will gratefully accept the incalculable comfort of such a belief to those sorrowing for precious friends hid in death's dateless night; he will acknowledge with gratitude and reverence the service to humanity of the great souls who have departed this life in a sure and certain hope—but this is all. Whether across death's threshold we step from life to life, or whether we go whence we shall not return, even to the land of darkness, as darkness itself, he cannot tell." [14]

The career of the famous scientist and inventor, Professor Michael Idvorsky Pupin, is dramatic and colourful. Pupin came to America from Serbia in March, 1874, when he was just a few months past his fifteenth birthday. Poor, lonely and homesick he was glad to lean against the smokestack of the vessel which brought him over in order to protect himself

---

[14] *Counsels and Ideals*, p. 254.

from the force of the gale and the sharpness of its icy blast. He landed in New York with five cents in his pocket and unable to speak one word of the English language. His rise to fame reads like a fairy tale, for in 1879, just five years after his arrival, this formerly penniless, friendless and ignorant boy was enrolled as a student in Columbia University. After a creditable career there he pursued further studies at Cambridge University in England and at the University of Berlin, Germany. In 1889 he became a teacher in the Department of Electrical Engineering in Columbia University. For almost a generation Michael Pupin has been regarded as one of the world's foremost authorities on the science of electrical engineering and kindred subjects. He has been a great inventor, and it is admitted that one invention alone saved for the American Telephone and Telegraph Company at least one hundred million dollars. The list of degrees and distinctions conferred upon him by centres of learning is a lengthy one. Professor Pupin believes emphatically that science and religion are complementary.

In much the same way as Henry Drummond, two generations ago, saw harmony in what was called at that time the natural and the spiritual world, the scientific investigations of Michael Pupin have all served to deepen his faith in a spiritual reality. This is how he sums up his faith in *The New Reformation* (page 271):

"Our Christian faith sees in the life and teaching of Jesus the highest spiritual reality which our belief in God, source of all spiritual realities, planted in the soul of man. This reality, we believe, endowed our souls with the spiritual forces which

guide us in the spiritual co-ordination of each individual life
and of the life of humanity. Love, according to Christ, is
the most powerful of all these co-ordinating forces. Its
action in the spiritual world is very similar to the action of
gravitational force in the physical world. Christ discovered
it and revealed it to us in His two commandments: 'Thou
shalt love the Lord thy God with all thy heart, and with all
thy soul, and with all thy mind. Thou shalt love thy neigh-
bor as thyself.'

"These two commandments are the fundamental law in
Christ's spiritual dynamics. It is obvious that under the
guidance of this law we can liberate ourselves from the dom-
inating love of purely material things and thus rescue our
own individual lives and the life of humanity from the threat-
ening chaos, and transform it into that life of simple law and
beautiful order.

"Creative co-ordination leads, therefore, to a higher level
of creation by the action of spiritual forces, just as it does
in the physical world by the action of physical forces. It is
the concept of this universal co-ordinating process which
unites the two worlds to each other, so that our understanding
of one will aid our understanding of the other. The cultiva-
tion of this view is encouraged by St. Paul: 'For the invisible
things of Him from the creation of the world are clearly
seen, being understood by the things that are made, even His
eternal power and Godhead.'

"Yes, God's spiritual realities are invisible; but they are
illustrated and made intelligible by the physical realities
revealed in the physical things which are made. According

to this interpretation of the Apostle's words the physical and the spiritual realities supplement each other. They are the two terminals of the same realities; one terminal residing in the human soul, and the other in the things of the external world. Here is one of the fundamental reasons why Science and Religion supplement each other. They are the two pillars of the portal through which the human soul enters the world where the divinity resides. If the signs of the time do not deceive then there is a universal drift towards this mental attitude.

"This drift I call The New Reformation." [15]

As might be expected, the thinking of Michael Pupin had undergone great changes from the time he lived in the village of Idvor in Serbia until he became one of the world's greatest inventors and scientists. His earliest memories are of simple-minded Serbian peasants and their conversations around the stove of his father's home on winter evenings. Yet Pupin made the change without losing any of the essence of that simple faith which came to him in his early years. Concerning those beliefs this is what he writes:

"Fifty years ago, instructed by David's psalms, I found in the light of the stars a heavenly language which proclaims the glory of God, but I did not know how that language reached me, and I hoped that some day I might find out. That hope was in my soul when I landed at Castle Garden. Today science tells me that the stars themselves bring it to me. Each burning star is a focus of energy, of life-giving acivity, which

---

[15] Michael Pupin, *The New Reformation.*

it pours out lavishly into every direction of the energy-hungry space; it pours out the life of its own heart, in order to beget new life. Oh, what a beautiful vista that opens to our imagination, and what new beauties are disclosed by science in the meaning of the words in Genesis: 'He breathed into his nostrils the breath of life, and man became a living soul.' The light of the stars is a part of the life-giving breath of God. I never look now upon the starlit vault of the heaven without feeling this divine breath and its quickening action upon my soul." [16]

Sir J. Arthur Thomson has been interested in the implications of religion in the field of science for more than twenty-five years. He is the author of a number of widely-known books, among them *The Bible of Nature, Darwinism in Human Life, The Gospel of Evolution, Modern Science,* and perhaps the best known work of all, *The Outline of Science.* He has been lecturer at many universities on both sides of the Atlantic, and at the time of writing is one of the foremost living scientists. He believes that science and religion would have had much more in common had it not been for hasty presentations of very young scientists on one hand, and dogmatic and unreasonable positions of theologians on the other. He writes:

"Often, of course, this supposed controversy is not a scientific controversy at all, but a thrust and parry between a hasty scientific generalization on one hand, and an unplastic theological conviction on the other."

---

[16] Michael Pupin, *From Immigrant to Inventor*, p. 381.

In a symposium of modern scientific opinion by Edward
H. Cotton, *Has Science Discovered God?*, Sir Arthur Thomson writes:

"Science aims at a description of things and processes in
terms of the Lowest Common Denominators available, while
Theology and the intellectual activities of Religion aim to
some transcendental interpretation, in which the highest concept is that of a Supreme Spiritual Reality—God. Between
the scientific description and the religious interpretation there
should be no antithesis, for they belong to different universes
of discourse, yet they must be consistent, for we cannot tolerate idea-tight compartments in our minds. Thus there
arise such questions as this article raises: how our theological
or religious ideas must undergo some modification as science
advances. This is surely as it should be if the world is in
any sense God's handiwork." [17]

Later in the same book (page 179) he deals with the whole
question of the religious significance of the evolutionist
theory, and ends by saying:

"The evolutionist vision sees a Creative Purpose that so
endowed the primitive irreducibles that the first organisms
included for all their descendants freedom to evolve in a
progressive way, expressing, without subsequently interpolated direction, more and more of the riches of reality—a
process of evolution that is still going on. This wider concept
of Creative Design is expressed in the words that Charles
Kingsley, in his 'Water Babies,' put into Dame Nature's

---

[17] *Has Science Discovered God?* p. 168.

mouth, as she sat with folded hands, so puzzlingly at leisure: 'You see, I make things make themselves.' Thus did the genius of the Creator save the evolving world from the shackles of determinism—leaving room for the freedom of individuality, and yet secured the climax in the first act of the drama. But this view has to be philosophically and religiously combined with the belief that created Nature, though superficially sufficient unto itself, is never out of the thoughts of Him in whom, in some inconceivable way, it lives and moves and has its being."

Amongst the present-day scientific teachers who are applying scientific facts to metaphysical reasoning, Sir James Jeans has a prominent place. Born in London in 1877, he received his academic training at Trinity College, Cambridge, and has been a lecturer in Applied Mathematics at Princeton University and at the University of Cambridge. His books *The Universe Around Us* and *The Mysterious Universe* have reached enormous unprecedented sale for works of that kind. With Arthur S. Eddington he must be regarded as one of the best known men of modern science. He utterly repudiates the materialistic interpretation of the universe. He refers repeatedly to the work of the Supreme Architect, the Master Mathematician. In *The Mysterious Universe* (page 122) he writes:

"We have already considered with disfavour the possibility of the universe having been planned by a biologist or an engineer. From the intrinsic evidence of his creation, the

Great Architect of the Universe now begins to appear as a pure mathematician."

In the same book (page 133) Sir James Jeans makes the following statement:

"If the universe is a universe of thought, then its creation must have been an act of thought. Indeed, the finiteness of time and space almost compel us, of themselves, to paint the creation as an act of thought; the determination of the constants such as the radius of the universe and the number of electrons it contained imply thought, whose richness is measured by the immensity of these quantities. Time and space, which form the setting for the thought, must have come into being as part of this act. Primitive cosmologies pictured a creator working in space and time, forging sun, moon and stars out of already existent raw material. Modern scientific theory compels us to think of the creator as working outside time and space, which are parts of his creation, just as the artist is outside his canvas. And yet, so little do we understand time that perhaps we ought to compare the whole of time to the act of creation, the materialisation of the thought."

No man has made a greater contribution to modern scientific progress than Thomas Alva Edison; the list of his inventions would occupy several pages of a book. For more than a generation he had no serious competitor as an inventor. When he died a few years ago tributes were paid to him by leading scientists in every country, and Sir Oliver Lodge placed him among, "The greatest beings of the world." His amazing concentration in scientific research—he frequently worked twenty hours a day—might have dulled his spiritual sensibilities, but this did not happen. He had clear religious views, intensely practical, but quite definite.

"Edison's scientific mind could not conceive of a universe so mathematically accurate without a guiding force or 'captain on the bridge of the ship.' The planets on their courses through the millions of years—the wonders of the earth with its multitudinous forms of life—the marvels of botany, geology, biology, all proved to him there was a supreme and ruling intelligence behind it.

"In a discussion with George Parsons Lathrop, he said: 'To me it seems that every atom is possessed by a certain amount of primitive intelligence. Look at the thousand ways in which atoms of hydrogen combine with those of other elements to form ᵗhe most diverse substances. Do you mean to say that they do this without intelligence?'

" 'Where does this intelligence come from?' asked Lathrop.

" 'From some power greater than ourselves,' replied Edison.

" 'Do you believe then in an Intelligent Creator—a personal God?'

" 'Certainly! The existence of such a God can, to my mind, almost be proved from chemistry.'

"Edison had a well-defined religion, which conformed to the strictest tenets of principles and ethics. He was familiar with all the philosophies of religions and believed that they all set up postulates that were provable in fact, although he did not conform with all the physical concepts of these spiritual realities. He was familiar with the Bible and with the scriptural teachings of other religions, and considered them 'the greatest rules of human conduct ever set up for man.' He did not see how man could live without them, as he required these guideposts to direct his way; therefore he confirmed the necessity of the church and the great work it has accomplished.

"His family made this statement: 'Although he subscribed to no orthodox creed, no one who knew him could have doubted his belief in, and reverence for, a Supreme Intelligence, and in his whole life the ideal of honest, loving service to his fellow men was predominant.' There is a letter in existence which he wrote on the stationery of his laboratory at Orange, in which he states: 'I believe in the existence of a Supreme Intelligence pervading the universe.' " [18]

In 1923 the American scientist, Robert Andrews Millikan, was awarded the Nobel Prize in physics for isolating and measuring the ultimate unit, the electron, and for photo-electric researches. In addition, he has received a great many honours from societies which encourage the arts and sciences. He is the author of many volumes treating of physics and related subjects. Dr. Millikan has been greatly interested in the relations existing between science and religion and has written and lectured extensively on the subject. He is an active layman in the Union Liberal Church, Pasadena, California.

Dr. Millikan is of the opinion that modern science is def-

---

[18] Francis Trevelyan Miller, *Thomas A. Edison Benefactor of Mankind*, pp. 292 and 293.

initely assisting religion. He writes: "No conception of God which has ever come into human thinking has been half so productive of effort on the part of man to change bad conditions as has this new modern conception that man himself plays a part in the scheme of evolution; this conception that has arisen because of work like that of Galileo, like that of Pasteur, and especially like that of Franklin and Faraday, that it is possible in increasing measure for us to know and to control, nature. This conception has inevitably been introduced into human thinking by the stupendous strides which have been made in the past century. And there are perhaps limitless possibilities ahead through the use of the scientific method for the enrichment of life and the development of the race.

"In this sense the idea that nature is at bottom benevolent has now become well-nigh universal. It is a contribution of science to religion, and a powerful extension or modification of the idea that Jesus saw so clearly and preached so persistently. He had felt that benevolence, and then preached it among men. Modern science has brought forward evidence for its belief. True, it has changed somewhat the conception and the emphasis, as was to have been expected, for it is this constant change in conception with the advance of thought and of knowledge that we are here attempting to follow. But the practical preaching of modern science—and it is the most insistent and effective preacher in the world today—is extraordinarily like the preaching of Jesus." [19]

---

[19] Robert Millikan, *The Evolution of Science and Religion*, p. 81.

Belonging to a decidedly liberal school, Millikan believes that true religion is indestructible although he has little patience either with dogmatic theologians or hidebound scientists. He believes that man is naturally and incurably religious. As witness the following: "It is not a question of whether one is religious or irreligious, so much as whether one is scientific or unscientific, rational or irrational. The world is of course 'incurably religious.' Why? Because every one who reflects at all must have conceptions about the world which go beyond the field of science, that is, beyond the present range of intellectual knowledge. As soon as we get beyond that range we are in the field that belongs to religion, and no one knows better than the man who works in science how soon we get beyond the boundaries of the known.

"These boundaries are continually changing, and so the conceptions that must start from them and have their footings in them are likewise of necessity changing. That is, religion is changing now, because of the interplay of science upon it, precisely as it has been changing in the past, and especially during the past century.

"There is a religion—one which keeps its mind continually open to new truth, which realizes that religion itself has continually undergone an evolution, that as our religious conceptions have changed in the past so they may be expected to change in the future; that eternal truth has been discovered in the past, that it is being discovered now, and will continue to be discovered. That kind of religion adapts itself to a growing, developing world.

"Physics has recently learned its lesson; and it has something to teach both philosophy and religion, namely, the lesson of not taking itself too seriously, not imagining that the human mind yet understands, or has made more than the barest beginning towards understanding the universe. Today physics is much more open-minded, much less dogmatic, much less disposed to make all-inclusive generalizations, and to imagine that it is dealing with ultimate realities, than it was twenty-five years ago. This generalizing further than the observed facts warrant; this tendency to assume that our finite minds have at any time attained to a complete understanding even of the basis of the physical universe, this sort of blunder has been made over and over again in all periods of the world's history, and in all domains of thought. It has been the chief sin of philosophy, the gravest error of religion, and the worst stupidity of science—this assumption of unpossessed knowledge, this dogmatic assertiveness, sometimes positive, sometimes negative, about matters concerning which we have no knowledge.

"If, as we pass from the seven-year-old to the thirty-year-old stage of our racial development, our conceptions of God become less childishly simple, more vague and indefinite, it is because we begin to realize that our finite minds have only just begun to touch the borders of the ocean of knowledge and understanding. 'Canst thou by searching find out God?'

"The prophet Micah said, twenty-five hundred years ago, 'What doth the Lord require of thee but to do justice, to love mercy, and to walk humbly with thy God?' Modern science of the real sort is learning to walk humbly with its

God. And in learning that lesson it is contributing something to religion." [20]

We complete this brief summary of scientific opinion with a reference to Arthur Stanley Eddington who since 1914 has been Plumian Professor of Astronomy at Cambridge University, England. He has been President of the Royal Astronomical Society and Chief-Assistant at the Royal Observatory in Greenwich. His epoch-making book *The Nature of the Physical World* was first published in 1928. In that work he made a definite break with those scientists who advocated the mechanistic theory of the universe. He vigorously and consistently advocates that behind all cosmic phenomena there is intelligent purpose and direction. There is a domain of life, he points out, in which science is not competent to pass judgement. He says:

"Let science pause before rushing in to apply a supposed scientific test; for such a test would go much too far, stripping away from our lives not only our religion but all our feelings which do not belong to the function of a measuring machine."

In *The Nature of the Physical World* (page 351), he says:

"A belief, not by any means confined to the more dogmatic adherents of religion is that there is a future non-material existence in store for us. Heaven is nowhere in space, but it is in time. (All the meaning of the belief is bound up with the word future; there is no comfort in an assurance of bliss in some former state of existence.) On the other hand the

---

[20] Robert A. Millikan, *The Evolution of Science and Religion*, p. 85.

scientist declares that time and space are a single continuum; and the modern idea of a Heaven in time but not in space is in this respect more at variance with science than the pre-Copernican idea of a Heaven above our heads. The question I am now putting is not whether the theologian or the scientist is right; but which is trespassing on the domain of the other. Cannot theology dispose of the destinies of the human soul in a non-material way without trespassing on the real of science? Cannot science assert its conclusions as to the geometry of the space-time continuum without trespassing on the realm of theology? According to the above assertion science and theology can make what mistakes they please provided that they make them *in their own territory.* They cannot quarrel if they keep to their own realms. But it will require a skillful drawing of the boundary line to frustrate the development of a conflict here."

Eddington, who is a member of the Society of Friends, repeatedly expresses the view that while creeds change, the deep spiritual experiences of religion remain. This is emphatically set forth in the following paragraph, with which he concludes his book, *Science and the Unseen World:*

"Rejection of creed is not inconsistent with being possessed by a living belief. We have no creed in science, but we are not lukewarm in our beliefs. The belief is not that all the knowledge of the universe that we hold so enthusiastically will survive in the letter; but a sureness that we are on the road. If our so-called facts are changing shadows, they are shadows cast by the light of constant truth. So too in religion we are repelled by that confident theological doctrine which has settled for all generations just how the spiritual world is worked; but we need not turn aside from the measure of light that comes into our experience showing us a Way through the unseen world. Religion for the conscientious seeker is not all a matter of doubt and self-questionings. There is a kind of sureness which is very different from cock-sureness."

CHAPTER NINE

Religious Faith of Great Soldiers

THE English historian, J. R. Green, says that "Alfred the Great furnishes the first instance in the history of Christendom of the Christian king; of a ruler who put aside every personal aim or ambition to devote himself to the welfare of those whom he ruled." "He combined as no other man has ever combined its practical energy, its patient and enduring force, its profound sense of duty, the reserve and self-control that steadies in it a wide outlook and a restless daring, its temperance and fairness, its frank geniality, its sensitiveness to action, its poetic tenderness, its deep and passionate religion.

Religion was the groundwork of Alfred's character. His temper was instinct with piety. Everywhere throughout his writings that remain to us the name of God, the thought of God, stir him to outbursts of ecstatic adoration. But he was no mere saint. He felt none of that scorn of the world about him which drove the nobler souls of his day to monastery or hermitage. Vexed as he was by sickness and constant pain, his temper took no touch of asceticism. His rare geniality, a peculiar elasticity and mobility of nature, gave colour and charm to his life. A sunny frankness and openness of spirit breathes in the pleasant chat of his books, and

what he was in his books he showed himself in his daily converse." [1] In many respects Alfred was a man of war; in
the very nature of the case he had to be, yet of his personal
piety and steadfast faith in God there is no doubt. In
Private Prayer in Christian Story, Jane T. Stoddart quotes
from Asser, a contemporary of King Alfred, this testimony:
"The King heard the divine offices daily. He observed the
services of the hours by day and by night, and oftentimes
was he wont, without the knowledge of his men, to go in the
night-time to the churches for the sake of prayer."

"William the Conqueror showed strange touches of a
humanity far in advance of his age," says J. R. Green, "con-
trasted with the general temper of his government. One of
the strongest traits in his character was his aversion to shed
blood by process of law; he formally abolished the punishment of death, and only a single execution stains the annals
of his reign. An edict yet more honourable to him put an
end to the slave trade which had till then been carried on at
the port of Bristol. If he was stark to baron or rebel he was
'mild to them that loved God.' "

The Conqueror passed away with words of prayer. Dean
Church thus describes his deathbed: "At early dawn on the
9th of September, 1087, from the abbey of St. Gervais outside of Rouen, whither he had been carried to be out of the
noise of the city, he heard the great bell of the cathedral
sound. He asked what it meant, and he was told that the bell
was going for prime in St. Mary's Church. 'Then the King

_____
[1] J. R. Green, *History of the English People,* p. 83.

raised his eyes to heaven, and, stretching out his arms, commended himself to his Lady, Mary the holy mother of God, that she by her holy intercession, would reconcile him to her dear Son, Christ; and he at once expired.' The physicians who had watched him all night, lying quiet without any sound of pain, were taken by surprise by the suddenness of his passing away, and 'became almost out of their mind.' " [2]

Soldiers of the Puritan age, whether followers of Cromwell, or supporters of the monarchy, were in many respects men of deep religious conviction. In some respects, they resembled the fighting heroes of the Old Testament. A striking example of this is found in the case of Sir Jacob Astley, one of the Royalist leaders at the battle of Edgehill, fought on October 28, 1642. Before the fighting opened, Sir Jacob prayed: "O Lord, Thou knowest how busy I must be this day. If I forget Thee, do not Thou forget me."

Of the religious faith of Oliver Cromwell, there is abundant evidence. In peace or in war, he was first, last and always a deeply religious man.

In September, 1643, Cromwell wrote: "A few honest men are better than numbers . . . if you choose godly honest men to be captains of horse, honest men will follow them. . . . I had rather have a plain russet-coated captain that knows what he fights for, and loves what he knows, than what you call a gentleman and nothing else. I honour a gentleman that is so indeed . . . it much concerns your good to have conscientous men." To his son, Henry Cromwell, he wrote:

---

[2] Jane T. Stoddart, *Private Prayer in Christian Story,* p. 57.

"I am glad to hear what I have of your courage; study still to be innocent; and to answer of occasion, roll yourself upon God, which to do needs much grace. Cry to the Lord to give you a plain simple heart."

Cromwell has been repeatedly accused of intolerance and religious fanaticism. That some of these attacks are well-founded is beyond question but it was an age of bitter religious controversy and the Puritans were driven to exasperation by their enemies. He felt himself as much called upon to deliver the nation from a cruel despotism as any man ever felt himself called to preach the Gospel. After the great victory at Marston Moor he wrote a letter to Colonel Valentine Walton, in which he said: "Truly England and the Church of God hath had a great favour from the Lord in this great victory given unto us, such as the like never was since this war began. It had all the evidences of an absolute victory obtained by the Lord's blessing upon the godly party principally. We never charged but we routed the enemy. The left wing, which I commanded, being our own horse, saving a few Scots in our rear, bent all the Prince's horse. God made them as stubble to our swords. . . . I believe of twenty thousand the Prince hath not four thousand left. Give glory, all the glory, to God." [8]

In 1645, after the storming of Bristol, he wrote to William Lenthall, Speaker of the Commons: "Thus I have given you a true, but not a full, account of this great business; wherein he that runs may read, that all this is none other than

---

[8] G. R. S. Taylor, *Cromwell*, p. 158.

the work of God. He must be a very atheist that doth not acknowledge it." When, at the close of the battle of Dunbar, the tide definitely turned in Cromwell's favour, Major Hodgson, who was near Cromwell, heard him say, "They run, they run. . . . Let God arise, let His enemies be scattered."

There was a very tender side to Cromwell which has often been lost sight of. In the letter to Colonel Walton, partly quoted above, he sought to console the stricken father for the loss of his son who had been slain at Marston Moor. He wrote: "God hath taken away your eldest son by a cannon-shot. You know my own trials this way, but the Lord supported me. I remember that my boy had entered into the happiness we all pant for and live for. There, too, is your precious child, full of glory, never to know sin or sorrow any more. He was a gallant young man, exceedingly gracious. God give you his comfort. You may do all things through Christ that strengtheneth us. Seek that, and you shall easily bear your trial. The Lord is your strength."

John Hampden, fellow-soldier and friend of Cromwell's, while equally vigorous in his battle for freedom never drew upon himself the hatred which his enemies felt for the Protector. Historians, sometimes harsh and bitter in their treatment of Cromwell, have been almost unanimous in their admiration of Hampden. Even King Charles I, against whom he fought so bitterly, was grieved to learn of John Hampden's death.

The records of that day, although written by men who were

his enemies in the war, thus chronicle his death: "The loss of Colonel Hampden goeth near the heart of every man that loves the good of his king and country. The memory of this deceased colonel is such that, in every age to come, it will more and more be held in honour and esteem; a man so religious and of that prudence, judgement, temper, valour, and integrity, that he hath left few his like behind him."

"We find him writing, at the age of thirty-seven, to Sir John Eliot. Sir John is troubled because his elder son has set his heart on going to France; the father dreads lest his boy should fall under pernicious influences there. John Hampden bids him be of good comfort. The father has done his best for the lad; let him leave the rest in higher hands. 'Then shall he be sure to find in France Him whom Abraham found in Sychem, and whom Joseph found in Egypt, under whose wing alone is perfect safety.' " [4]

"Few pages in our annals are more affecting than those which describe the death of Hampden. With his head bending down, and his hands resting on his horse's neck, he was seen riding off the field before the action was done—'a thing,' says Lord Clarendon, 'he never used to do, and from which it was concluded that he was hurt.' He turned his horse's head towards the lovely home at which he had wooed and won the bride of his youth; but, cut off by hostile troops, he changed his mind and rode in another direction. His strength fast failing, he was taken to a cottager's home to die. For six days he occupied himself, though in excruciating agony,

---

[4] F. W. Boreham, *A Faggot of Torches,* pp. 112 and 117.

in giving instructions concerning the disposal of public affairs. Just before the end he took the Lord's Supper, and then, thoroughly spent, he turned his face to the wall that he might die in prayer.

" 'O Lord of Hosts,' he was heard to say, 'great is Thy mercy; just and holy are Thy dealings with us sinful men. Pardon, O Lord, my manifold transgressions. O Lord, save my bleeding country. Have these realms in Thy special keeping. Let the King see his error; and turn the hearts of his councillors from the malice and wickedness of their designs. Lord Jesus, receive my spirit!'

"There was a pause. And then, in a feebler voice, he continued: 'O Lord, save my country; *O Lord, be merciful to—*' But here speech failed him. He fell back in the bed and expired."

In a letter to Lady Webster a few hours after the Battle of Waterloo, the Duke of Wellington said: "The Finger of Providence was upon me and I escaped unhurt." Doubtless this indicated religious faith but a study of Wellington's life shows that he never fully understood the deeper significance of the Christian religion.

He approved of the church and according to one historian he, "professed implicit and uncompromising belief in the doctrines of the Church," but one suspects he had more regard for the Church as a national institution than he had understanding of its mystical message.

"Bishop Philpotts wrote to him in 1833 reminding him how he 'might do honour to God, and by His grace much spiritual good to men, by setting the example of regular attendance at public worship.' Wellington replied in a long letter published in the *Civil Despatches,* in which he declares he is particularly anxious to remove from the bishop's mind 'the notion that I am a person without any sense of religion. If I am so,' says Wellington, 'I am unpardonable.' He goes on to say, 'I do not make much show or boast on any subject; I never have done so. I am not a "Bible Society man" upon principle, and I make no ostentatious display either of charity or of other Christian virtues, though I believe that, besides enormous sums given to hundreds and thousands who have positive claims upon me, there is not a charity of any description within my reach to which I am not a contributor.'

"Wellington explains that he goes to church whenever his presence can operate as an example; but he explains that he is deaf, and cannot hear the sermon; that to sit for hours in a cold church would increase his deafness; and he adds:

" 'But excepting that duty, which I never fail to perform in the country, I don't know of any that I leave unperformed. There is room for amendment in every man, in me as well as in others; and there is nothing better calculated to inspire such amendment than such a letter as that from your Lordship.' " [5]

While this letter reveals 'Wellington's regard for the externals of religion it seems unfair to surmise, as one biographer does, that "Of the mystical, or rather, spiritual side of

---

[5] W. H. Fitchett, *The Great Duke,* Volume II, p. 387.

religion—of its great emotions, its conception of the soul's personal relationship with God, and of man as a fallen creature of God, shut in within a circle of redemptive forces— Wellington knew nothing." [6]

He was never religious in the sense that General Gordon was; he never felt called upon to promote vital religion among the soldiers as did Stonewall Jackson, nevertheless he had a measure of religious faith which he never lost. "When at Strathfieldsaye he regularly partook of the Lord's Supper, and, says Gleig, 'it was a touching sight to see that great and venerable man kneeling devoutly before the altar-rails of the village church with the sunlight falling through the stained glass upon his head.'"

More biographies of Napoleon Bonaparte have been written than of almost any other man. His attitude towards religion is uncertain—not because he did not express himself freely on the subject but because he expressed himself so often. He talked in different ways at different times and to different people. "In particular it should be noted, for the fact is itself characteristic, the opinions which he gave out for consumption were often hopelessly at variance with those which he expressed in confidential intercourse."

"He had a profound sense of the political value of religion. This is only what we should expect in the author of the Concordat. 'Religion is useful to mankind,' he said. 'Those who govern should employ it to influence men'—a typical bit of Machiavellism. But even at the time of the Concordat he

---

⁶ W. H. Fitchett, *The Great Duke*, Volume II, p. 388.

disclaimed any personal interest in the restored faith: 'For this, some will call me a papist. I am no such thing. I am no believer in creed. I was a Mohammedan in Egypt. I am a Catholic in France.' Once again we recognise the Superman's calm contempt for what he nevertheless deems excellent for the masses. Yet for the sake of policy he kept up the outward show of conformity to the church, and was solicitous lest his private views should interfere with the effectiveness of his public action. . . .

"Thus regarding religion as a political instrument he held fast to the Roman Church. Protestantism he considered as a source of dissensions, and therefore of trouble to the government. Moreover—and here again we have the Superman—he believed it to be an advantage that in the Roman Church the majority of the people do not understand their prayers: it is better that they should not understand too much about such things! Yet, very naturally, he was hostile to the Papacy, as an illegitimate rival to civil authority. . . .

"His attitude towards Christianity varied, but it was often openly antagonistic. Jesus he treated as a mere fanatic, who set up for the Messiah, and met a fanatic's well-deserved fate. In regard to man he was entirely materialist, and repudiated the doctrine of the immortality of the soul. Nor had he, as I have said, any faith in the providential ordering of the world. These at least are the conclusions stated by him in familiar conversations and in terms which seem precise enough to be accepted as final. It may be, however, as Lord Rosebery surmises, that Napoleon at the bottom of his heart was more deeply impressed by the mystery which religion offers to faith, than such conversational utterances would lead us to infer. Certain it is that in his years of exile religion was continually in his mind. Certain it is too that he never wholly escaped from the associations of the Catholicism in which he had been bred. He was, we are told, always moved by the sound of church bells. Superstitious rather than devout, he involuntarily crossed himself at every moment of crisis or special peril. It was by his own directions, as we have seen, that the rites of extreme unction were administered at the end." [7]

On St. Helena his mind turned increasingly to the subject of religion, and more and more he abandoned the materialistic philosophy for theism. To Laplace, who denied the existence of God, he said: "You should be more ready than any one else to admit that God exists, for you, more than most, have seen the wonders of creation. If we cannot actually see God with our own eyes, this is because he did not wish our understanding to reach so far." On another occasion: "We believe in God because everything around us testifies to his existence." In St. Helena: "I have never doubted the existence of God, for, even if my reason were incompetent to grasp Him, still my inner feelings would convince me of his reality. My temperament has always been in harmony with this feeling." [8]

During his closing years he insisted that he was an instrument in the hands of God, doing His will. To the Duchess of Weimar he said: "Believe me, there is a providence which

---

[7] W. H. Hudson, *The Man Napoleon*, pp. 225-228.
[8] Emil Ludwig, *Napoleon*, p. 602.

guides all. I am merely its instrument." With pathetic emphasis he sought to justify his career; maintaining that he had never been the aggressor in any way.

Two weeks before his death he sent for a Corsican priest. He wished to be prepared for the end. There was probably more superstition than religious faith. "After my death," he said, "you will set up your altar by my bedside, and will say Mass with the usual ceremonies until I am under ground." As the end drew near his sufferings became more acute. One day the priest visited him unsummoned. As he left the dying man's room he said, "I have given him extreme unction. Owing to the condition of his stomach, no other sacrament was possible." The following day Napoleon died.

In St. Paul's Cathedral, not many feet from the tomb of the Duke of Wellington, rests the body of General Gordon, a brave warrior, a true gentlemen and a devout Christian. The simple inscription on his monument there is singularly impressive: "At all times and everywhere, he gave his strength to the weak, his substance to the poor, his sympathy to the suffering, and his heart to God."

It was literally true that he gave his substance to the poor. When he was appointed Governor of the Equatorial Province, he cut down his pay from six thousand to two thousand pounds, saying that he could not bear to take money which would be wrung from the poor peasants. The sight of so many poor, unfortunate people in the East distressed him and no one will ever know how much he gave away. During the six years which he spent at Gravesend in command of the Royal Engineers, he gave both of his money and freely of his personal service to the suffering and the poor.

He worked in Sunday schools and took great pains to secure good posts for boys going to sea. He had a map on his wall marked with pins and little flags, showing the whereabouts of the boys: "I pray for each one of them, day by day," he said.

He hated war, which he described as "a brutal, cruel affair," and only a stern sense of duty made it possible for him to fight, but, once convinced that he was right, he seemed to be utterly without fear. He remained equally unmoved in face of physical danger or the opposition and ridicule of men. He was calm, placid, under circumstances which would have unnerved and broken down even strong men.

The most conspicuous thing about Gordon was his religious faith. Largely influenced by his sister, he became a Christian in early manhood, and throughout the thrilling experiences of his eventful life he remained true to Jesus Christ. He once said that, during his early experiences in China, his faith became obscured, but an attack of smallpox steadied him. "I am glad to say," he wrote to his sister, "that this disease has brought me back to my Saviour, and I trust in the future to be a better Christian than I have been heretofore."

General Gordon was an assiduous tract distributor. Any one who ever followed him found abundant evidence of this. If there were a stile to be got over, a tract would be left, held down by a stone. In the path at intervals, other tracts would be left in the same way. Sometimes they would be nailed to fences or trees. There was much good-natured joking among the soldiers over his tract distributing, but it is questionable whether any other soldier ever left the same deep impression for good upon those with whom he came in contact as did "Chinese Gordon," as he was so often called.

He believed in personal evangelism. His favorite verse of Scripture was: "Whosoever shall confess that Jesus is the Son of God, God dwelleth in him, and he in God." When he left England for the last time, he presented every member of the British Cabinet with a copy of Dr. Samuel Clarke's "Scripture Promises," a book which had greatly helped him. He was a member of the Church of England but actually he belonged to all churches. He had a deep and enthusiastic interest in missions and it was characteristic of him that he should say to the missionary authorities: "Do not send luke-warm men to the mission field." Gordon might well write this, for few men have been so whole-heartedly devoted to God as he.

Of that Christian soldier, General Stonewall Jackson, his biographer, Colonel G. F. R. Henderson, writes: "He prayed without ceasing, under fire as in the camp; but he never mistook his own impulse for a revelation of the Divine will. He prayed for help to do his duty, and he prayed for success, . . . but he knew that prayer is not always answered in the way that man would have it."

In his tent at night, during the Civil War, General Jackson and his staff "gathered together for their evening devotions, and the conversation ran not on the merits of horse and hound, on strategy or tactics, but on the power of faith and the mysteries of redemption." After the battle of Bull Run a brother officer said to him: "General, how is it that you can keep so cool, and appear so utterly insensible to danger in such a storm of shell and bullets as rained about you when your hand was hit?" "He instantly became grave and reverential in his manner, and answered, in a low tone of great earnestness: 'Captain, my religious belief teaches me to feel as safe in battle as in bed. God has fixed the time for my death. I do not concern myself about that, but to be always ready, no matter when it may overtake me.' He added after a pause, looking me full in the face, 'That is the way all men should live, and then all would be equally brave.' " [9]

"His devout habits were no secret in the camp. Jim, most faithful of servants, declared that he could always tell when there was going to be a battle. 'The general,' he said, 'is a great man for prayin'. He pray night and mornin'—all times. But when I see him git up several times in the night, an' go off an' pray, *den I know there is goin' to be somethin' to pay,* an' I go right away and pack his haversack!' "

Stonewall Jackson "made no secret of his absolute dependence on a higher Power. Every action was a prayer, for every action was begun and ended in the name of the Almighty. Consciously and unconsciously, in deed as in word, in the quiet of his home and in the tumult of battle, he fastened to his soul those golden chains 'that bind the whole round earth about the feet of God.' Nor was their burden

---

[9] Jane T. Stoddart, *Private Prayer in Christian Story,* p. 283.

heavy. 'He was the happiest man,' says one of his friends, 'I ever knew,' and he was wont to express his surprise that others were less happy than himself." [10]

General Robert E. Lee won the most difficult of all battles; he overcame the prejudice of his enemies to such an extent that before his death he was probably as much esteemed in the North as in the South. The story of his life is too well-known to need repeating here but who can forget the closing years of that noble life, years in which he endeavoured in every possible way, to heal the wounds of his people.

Lee was profoundly religious; it is evidenced in everything he did. On August 13, 1863, he issued the following order:

"Headquarters, Army Northern Virginia,

"August 13, 1863.

"The President of the Confederate States has, in the name of the people, appointed August 21st as a day of fasting, humiliation, and prayer. A strict observance of the day is enjoined upon the officers and soldiers of this army. All military duties, except such as are absolutely necessary, will be suspended. The commanding officers of brigades and regiments are requested to cause divine services, suitable to the occasion, to be performed in their respective commands. Soldiers! we have sinned against Almighty God. We have forgotten His signal mercies, and have cultivated a revenge-

---

[10] G. F. R. Henderson, *Stonewall Jackson and the American Civil War*, Volume II, p. 610.

ful, haughty, and boastful spirit. We have not remembered that the defenders of a just cause should be pure in His eyes; that 'our times are in His hands,' and we have relied too much on our own arms for the achievement of our independence. God is our only refuge and our strength. Let us humble ourselves before Him. Let us confess our many sins, and beseech Him to give us a higher courage, a purer patriotism, and more determined will; that He will convert the hearts of our enemies; that He will hasten the time when war, with its sorrows and sufferings, shall cease, and that He will give us a name and place among the nations of the earth.

"R. E. Lee, General." [11]

General Lee was singularly free from cant and had little patience with sectarianism. It is said that during the Civil War a captain had refused permission to a Jewish soldier who wished to attend a synagogue. The general granted the man his request and firmly rebuked the captain and told him in future, "to respect the religious views and feelings of others."

Robert E. Page writes of Lee: "If possible, Lee was even more pious than Jackson. Both were men who, in the early prime of their manhood, consecrated themselves to God, and henceforth served him with a single heart. It shines forth in every page they ever penned. It was the basis of their character. No man can familiarize himself with Lee's life without seeing that he was a man consecrated to the service of his Divine Master, and amid all conditions possessed a

---

[11] His son, *Recollections of General Lee*, pp. 105-106.

mind stayed on him." It was fitting that Richard Keen's great hymn, "How Firm a Foundation," was sung at Lee's funeral.

General Ulysses S. Grant, one of the foremost generals during the Civil War and eighteenth President of the United States, is regarded, with Lincoln, as the saver of the Union. He had many admirable and lovable traits; kind, generous, sympathetic and possessing a strong sense of justice. He cannot be said to have been deeply religious, at least not in the same way as Jackson or Lee. A recent biographer writes: "His religion, such as it was, appears to have been a kind of ethical paganism. Like Washington, Lincoln, Franklin and Thomas Paine, Grant believed in God, but Grant's God was not the God of the Christians. He conceived the Deity as a dark, inscrutable Providence with mysterious ways and a tendency to interfere arbitrarily now and then in human affairs . . . a Providence that seems to be pretty nearly synonymous with Luck.

"According to M. J. Cramer, a preacher who married one of the General's sisters, Grant believed that 'all evil must be punished in some form at some time.' He went on—still according to Cramer—to say that 'as nations have no organized existence hereafter, they must be punished here for their national sins'—hence he looked upon the Civil War as a divine punishment for the sin of slavery.

"Cramer tried, apparently, to convert Grant and to induce him to become a member of the church, for he talked continually about religion with his famous brother-in-law. At one time he declared to Grant that he did not believe there was really an out-and-out atheist in the world, because religion— no matter what its form may be—is an innate, or an intuitive, element of man's soul, and all religious presuppose a deity, or deities, of some kind or other. To this Grant replied: 'Why, Mr. Cramer, I think your views are about right.' This is as near as he ever got to making a confession of religious faith.

"One of Grant's public statements leads one to the conviction that he considered God a pacifist and an internationalist, but a little slow in action. He said: 'I believe that our Great Maker is preparing this world in His own good time to become one nation, speaking one language, and when armies and navies will no longer be required.'" [12]

Later in the same volume in dealing with the closing scenes of Grant's life, Mr. Woodward writes, "He had a religion of his own, in which honorable conduct, truth and justice were the chief articles of faith. He was not an atheist. He believed in God and hoped for a future life. In his last letter to his wife he says something about meeting her in another world. He wrote this letter shortly before his death and put it in his pocket." [13]

---

[12] W. E. Woodward, *Meet General Grant,* pp. 369-370.
[13] *Ibid.,* p. 500.

CHAPTER TEN

Religious Faith of Great Statesmen

GEORGE WILLIAM CURTIS once asked this question: "Could Gladstone have swayed England with his fervent eloquence, as the moon moves the tides, if he had been a gambling, swearing, boozing squire?" To ask such a question is to answer it. Although he owed much to his great natural gifts, no one would dispute the saying of his biographer, John Morley: "Not for two centuries has Great Britain produced a ruler in whom the religious motive was paramount in like degree."

In 1818, when he was nine years of age, Gladstone's mother wrote to a friend: "I am quite sure that William has been truly converted to God." His influence for good at Eton was such that there were youths who acknowledged that their decision to study at Oxford was made in order to be near young Gladstone. When he reached the age of twenty-one he wrote in his diary that the greatest ambition of his life was to have the life of God the supreme habit of his soul.

Gladstone very nearly entered the ministry of the Church of England. It is interesting to speculate upon what might have been the result had he taken that step. "We cannot without hesitation join with those who lightly declare that it was altogether good that Gladstone should have been deterred by his father from taking this step. The Church in the last century sorely needed leadership. When we consider its present position, representing as it does the spirit of redemption and reconciliation in human life, and yet pathetically ineffective in this divine and most necessary ministry, we conjecture wistfully what might have been accomplished by that eager and powerful personality entirely engaged in its interests. To the end of his life, Gladstone realised the tremendous urgency and indispensableness of the work of the Christian Church. He was an old man when he wrote to the Duke of Argyll his deep conviction that 'we politicians are children playing with toys in comparison to that great work of and for mankind which has to be done and will yet be done, in restoring belief.' " [1]

"The world thought of Gladstone as a politician," said Lord Rosebery, into whose hands Mr. Gladstone relinquished the leadership. "To those of us who were privileged to enjoy his friendship, his politics seems but the least part of him. Indeed, I sometimes doubt whether his natural bent was towards politics at all. The predominating part, to which all else was subordinated, was his religion. An intimate and vital religious experience was the essence, the savour and the motive power of his whole life."

"He has left behind him," said Lord Salisbury, the Conservative Prime Minister, "he has left behind him the memory of a great Christian statesman. He will be remembered, not

---

[1] Trevor H. Davies, *Spiritual Voices in Modern Literature*, p. 200.

so much for the causes in which he was engaged, or the political projects which he favoured, but as an example, of which history hardly furnishes a parallel, of a great Christian man."

There is no need to write of Gladstone's extraordinary intellectual qualities. His political opponents were as willing to acknowledge these gifts as were his friends. For sixty-five years he was closely associated with many of the greatest minds of his age, yet there are those who would not hesitate to say that, in the richness and variety of his gifts and achievements, he was the peer of all his contemporaries.

The most striking thing about this "Matterhorn of Men" was his strong religious faith. He accepted Christ as his Saviour with the simplicity of a little child. All his serious thinking and research deepened his religious faith and strengthened his convictions.

One day a member of the House of Commons said: "You know, Mr. Speaker, we all believe in a God of some sort or another." This flippant remark aroused Gladstone's indignation. He thundered his protest: "I am not willing," he said, "that Christianity shall stand in any place lower than that which is indispensable." Throughout his life, while carrying burdens, which might have crushed strong men, he was sustained by his practice of prayer. He said he never could have overcome his extreme nervousness, but for the grace of God, and he rarely made an important speech without spending some time in silent prayer.

He died on the tenth of May, 1898. "I knelt by his death-bed," says the Bishop of St. Andrews, "and received his parting benediction. As I turned away, I felt I had been on the Mount of Transfiguration and had seen a glimpse of Paradise through the gates ajar."

John Bright was a contemporary of Gladstone. As a political force in Great Britain in the middle of last century, he stands in the first rank. He had a passion for righteous causes which burned at white heat and, coupled with this, was a remarkable gift of oratory. His transparent sincerity was such that, even when he opposed great causes, as, for instance, the Crimean War, all regarded him with respect which approached reverence.

He was a devout Quaker and although he differed with some of them on minor matters he remained loyal to their fellowship. "In London on Sunday he regularly throughout his life attended the Friends' Meeting in Westminster, and seldom omitted in writing to his wife later in the day to give the names of those who had offered prayer or spoken, often adding a brief summary of what had been said, with comments. He continued always to take a thoughtful interest in the doings of the Society both in the conduct of its business and in the position it took up on many public questions, with which as a rule he was in complete sympathy. He always remained a Friend both in his heart and in his life." [2]

When Bright's wife died in 1878 he received the following letter from Bishop Fraser of Manchester: "My Dear Sir,

---

[2] George M. Trevelyan, *Life of John Bright*, p. 414.

—May I, without being deemed an intruder upon the sanctities of sorrow, venture to offer you this simple, but heartfelt, expression of my sympathy and respect, under the heavy blow which has just befallen you.

"I have often heard your home life described not long ago by our common friend, E. J. Broadfield: and his picture of your household gathering together, and yourself reading the 103rd Psalm to them, is one that will not soon fade from my memory. I have rejoiced to think that it is only a type of many homes in England still uncontaminated by that fashion-service and world-worship, which seems to be almost eating out the old, honest heart of the nation.

"And she, whom you have lost, was part of this picture; and I can understand what the blank must be, now that she is gone. As a fellow Christian man, I pray that God may comfort you, and that you may still be able to say in those beautiful words which sank so deeply into Edward Broadfield's ears, as he heard you read them a few weeks ago, 'Praise the Lord, O my soul; and *forget not all His benefits.*'"

The Australian essayist, Rev. F. W. Boreham, writes: "Lord Morley speaking for himself confessed that 'the most pure and impressive piece of religion that he ever witnessed was John Bright reading a chapter of the Bible to his maid-servants shortly after his wife's death, in his beautiful and feeling voice, followed by a Quaker silence.' Lord Morley ranks John Bright with John Hampden, John Selden, John Pym and the great Puritans, men who, in Macaulay's classic phrase, 'were not content to catch occasional glimpses of the

Deity through an obscuring veil, but aspired to gaze full on
His intolerable brightness and commune with Him face to
face.' 'It was this,' says Lord Morley, 'that made John
Bright the glory of the House of Commons.' He sometimes
startled men by unexpectedly drawing the veil and revealing
the immanence of the unseen and eternal. Dr. Dale describes
one of his great orations. It was delivered in the Birming-
ham Town Hall. The chairs had been removed so that as
many as possible could be crowded into the building. Five
thousand men stood on the floor, packed so tightly that they
could not raise their hands from their sides to applaud. Mr.
Bright had recently been ill; and he began by reverently expressing his gratitude to God for his recovery. Dr. Dale
says that the hush that fell on the vast and excited assembly
as soon as he began to speak deepened into awe. 'We had
expected a fierce assault on his political opponents; but the
storms of party passion were for a moment stilled; we suddenly found ourselves in the presence of the eternal, and
some of us, perhaps, rebuked ourselves in the words of the
patriarch, *"Surely the Lord is in this place and I knew it
not!"* '[3]

Perhaps no other statesman has ever made such frequent
and effective use of the Bible as John Bright. He was no
faddist, but in a simple, direct, impressive manner, he knew
how to draw upon his amazing knowledge of the Scriptures.
He belonged to the sect of Quakers and throughout life
acknowledged the absolute supremacy of Jesus. In many

---

[3] F. W. Boreham, *A Casket of Cameos*, p. 106.

respects his life was a troubled one. He suffered a succession of heavy blows, but he bore them with Christian fortitude. His faith sustained him in hours of deepest need.

There is a passage in a letter written by Boswell in which he gives this description of the British statesman, William Wilberforce: "I saw a shrimp mount the table; but as I listened, he grew and grew, until the shrimp became a whale." Wilberforce had serious physical handicaps, so serious, that when he was a boy, his parents thought of his future with many misgivings. His career is a striking illustration of the soul's triumph over terrible odds. He exerted a great influence over his fellows and the way in which he championed noble causes made him one of the great moral forces of his generation.

"As a youth, preparing himself to play some worthy part in life, Wilberforce travels. Thrice he tours Europe, once in the company of William Pitt, then a young fellow of exactly his own age, and twice in the company of Isaac Milner, the brilliant brother of his Hull schoolmaster. It was in the course of one of these tours that the crisis of his inner life overtook him. Milner and he made it a practice to carry with them a few books to read on rainy days. Amongst these oddly-assorted volumes they slipped into their luggage a copy of Dr. Doddridge's *Rise and Progress of Religion in the Soul.* It was a dangerous companion for young men who prized their peace of mind; no book of that period had provoked more serious thought. It certainly set Wilberforce thinking; and not all the festivities of his tour nor the laughter of his friends could dispel the feeling that now took sole possession of his mind. One overpowering emotion drove out all others. It haunted him sleeping and waking. 'My sin!' he cried, 'my sin, my sin, my sin!' —it was this thought of his condition that filled him with apprehension and despair." [4]

Wilberforce belonged to that class of men who felt the exceeding sinfulness of sin. His own sense of unworthiness was constantly with him. His favorite text of Scripture, ever upon his lips, was the publican's prayer: "God be merciful to me."

Wilberforce solemnly dedicated his life to God, and he devoted his powers to fight for the emancipation of the slaves. Like Wolfe at Quebec, he received the news of victory as he was dying. The end was very near when messengers hurried into his room to tell him that the Emancipation Bill had been passed. What the dying statesman said was characteristic of him: "Thank God! that I have lived to see this day." Frail, misshapen; a dwarf in body, Wilberforce was a giant in mind and in soul. And it was his unfaltering faith in Jesus Christ which made him great.

Nothing could be more characteristic of the Prussian statesman, Bismarck, than his pronouncement on the Christian State:

"No State has a secure existence unless it has a religious foundation. For me, the words, 'by the Grace of God,' which Christian rulers add to their name, are no empty

---

[4] F. W. Boreham, *A Bunch of Everlastings*, p. 188.

phrase; I see in them a confession that the Princes desire to wield the sceptre which God has given them according to the will of God on earth. As the will of God I can only recognise that which has been revealed in the Christian Gospel—I believe that the realisation of Christian teaching is the end of the State; I do not believe that we shall more nearly approach this end by the help of the Jews. . . . If we withdraw this foundation, we retain in a State nothing but an accidental aggregate of rights, a kind of bulwark against the war of all against all, which ancient philosophy has assumed. Therefore, gentlemen, do not let us spoil the people of their Christianity; do not let us take from them the belief that our legislation is drawn from the well of Christianity, and that the State aims at the realisation of Christianity even if it does not attain its end." [5]

Although temperamentally sceptical and probably never a deeply religious man, Count Von Bismarck came under the influence of a religious movement led by Herr Von Thadden. This man started religious exercises in his own home which were attended not only by the peasants of the village but by many of the county gentry. These people had no intention of breaking away from Lutheran doctrine—on the contrary they urged its strictest enforcement—but they were dissatisfied with the rationalistic preaching of the clergy and they aimed at greater religious depth and feeling. Bismarck attended the meetings regularly and the religious impressions he received at that time never left him.

---

[5] James W. Headlam, *Bismarck,* p. 42.

"The religious convictions which Bismarck learnt from them were to be lasting, and they profoundly influenced his character. He had probably received little religious training from his mother, who belonged to the rationalistic school of thought. It was by them that his monarchical feeling was strengthened. It is not at first apparent what necessary connection there is between monarchical government and Christian faith. For Bismarck they were ever inseparably bound together; nothing but religious belief would have reconciled him to a form of government so repugnant to natural human reason. 'If I were not a Christian, I would be a Republican,' he said many years later; in Christianity he found the only support against revolution and socialism. He was not the man to be beguiled by romantic sentiment; he was not a courtier to be blinded by the pomp and ceremony of royalty; he was too stubborn and independent to acquiesce in the arbitrary rule of a single man. He could only obey the king if the king himself held his authority as the representative of a higher power. Bismarck was accustomed to follow out his thought to its conclusions. To whom did the king owe his power? There was only one alternative: to the people or to God. If to the people, then it was a mere question of convenience whether the monarchy were continued in form; there was little to choose between a constitutional monarchy where the king was appointed by the people and controlled by Parliament, and an avowed republic. This was the principle held by nearly all his contemporaries. He deliberately rejected it. He did not hold that the voice of the people was the voice of God. This belief did not satisfy his moral sense;

it seemed in public life to leave all to interest and ambition
and nothing to duty. It did not satisfy his critical intellect;
the word 'people' was to him a vague idea. The service of
the People or of the King by the Grace of God, this was the
struggle which was soon to be fought out." [6]

It was from amongst these Pietists that Bismarck found his
wife. He fell in love with Johanna von Puttkamer whom
Blanckenburg—Bismarck's most intimate friend—referred to
as a young woman with, "a serious and pious mind." The
letter Bismarck wrote to Johanna's father asking her hand
in marriage is full of pious expressions and had it been
sincere would indicate deep religious conviction. One is inclined to agree, however, with Emil Ludwig that Bismarck
was acting, "with the art of the born diplomatist—a letter
written to suit the pious mood of the recipient."

Once his proposal had been accepted Bismarck, who at
that time was thirty-two, wrote to his brother frankly stating
his religious views: "In matters of faith, we differ somewhat,
more to her distress than to mine. Still, the difference is not
so great as you might imagine, for many external and internal happenings have wrought changes in me of late, so
that now (a new thing in me, as you know) I feel justified
in numbering myself among those who believe in the Christian religion. Although in respect of some of the doctrines,
perhaps those which Christians as a rule consider the most
important, I am—so far as I am clear concerning my own
views—by no means fully reconciled with the Christian out-

* *Ibid.*, pp. 31 and 32.

look, nevertheless, tacitly as it were, a sort of Treaty of Passau has been signed between myself and Johanna. Besides, I like pietism in women, and detest members of the female sex who make a parade of enlightenment." [7]

Yet when Bismarck resigned from public office—a resignation forced upon him—his loneliness was pathetic. "Long ago, his Christianity had become a mere matter of form; now, it is over and done with. At the close of his life, as in the early days, his mind is dominated by a scepticism in which from time to time a sort of pagan mysticism shapes itself. The only man who can venture to question him about these matters, Keyserling, the friend of his youth, gives a sympathetic explanation: 'His religious sentiment' (the words are penned after Keyserling's last visit to his old friend) 'seems to have experienced ebbs and flows. . . .' Keyserling records, as Bismarck's last confession: 'I am sorry to say that during the struggles of the last two decades, I have moved away to a great distance from God. In these sad times, I find this severance painful.' " [8]

He was religious in much the same way as the Duke of Wellington. He believed in the Church but chiefly as a bulwark of the State. "His religion was not of that complexion that he could find in contemplation, and in preparation for another life, consolation for the trials of this one."

The great statesmen of the New World have often been,

[7] Emil Ludwig, *Bismarck*, p. 57.
[8] *Ibid.*, pp. 624-625.

like their fellows across the seas, men of deep religious faith. There is not room here to quote all we would wish of that letter which George Washington wrote to his wife in 1775, but this paragraph reveals how reverently he assumed his responsibilities: "You may believe me when I assure you, in the most solemn manner, that so far from seeking this employment, I have used every effort in my power to avoid it . . . I shall rely confidently on that Providence, which has heretofore preserved and been bountiful to me, not doubting but that I shall return to you in the fall."

One of the earliest biographers of Washington was Doctor David Ramsay, a celebrated physician of South Carolina and a delegate to the Continental Congress in 1782-86. In his biography he says: "There are few men of any kind, and still fewer of those the world calls great, who have not some of their virtues eclipsed by corresponding vices. But this was not the case with General Washington. He had religion without austerity, dignity without pride, modesty without diffidence, courage without rashness, politeness without affection, affability without familiarity. His private character, as well as his public one, will bear the strictest scrutiny. He was punctual in all his engagements; upright and honest in his dealings; temperate in his enjoyments; liberal and hospitable to an eminent degree; a lover of order; systematical and methodical in his arrangements. He was a friend of morality and religion; steadily attended on public worship; encouraged and strengthened the hands of the clergy. In all his public acts he made the most respectful mention of Provi-

dence; and, in a word, carried the spirit of piety with him
both in his private life and public administration." [9]

Washington had, to a very unusual degree, a sense of
God's presence wherever he went. There were times when
he appeared foolhardy, but it was due to this fact: he believed that God was taking care of him. After a disastrous
fight with Indians, early in his career, he wrote to his mother:
"The Virginian troops showed a great deal of bravery, and
were nearly all killed, for I believe that out of three com-
panies scarcely thirty men were left alive. By the all-powerful
dispensations of Providence I have been protected beyond all
human probability or expectation."

When the War of Independence came to a close on October
19, 1781, Washington issued orders for a general thanksgiving to God in these words: "The Commander-in-Chief
earnestly recommends that the troops not on duty should
universally attend, with the seriousness of deportment and
gratitude of heart, which the recognition of such reiterated
and astonishing interpositions of Providence demand of us."

If what Plato said is true, that the best rulers are those
who rule unwillingly, then Washington's success is not to be
wondered at. He did not seek office; he was sought. When
he was elected to the President's chair, amid scenes of great
enthusiasm, he went to Federal Hall to take the oath. There
he stood, before the throng, with his hand upon the open
Bible. Was it an accident that the hand of this deeply-

---

[9] Ramsay, *Life of Washington,* p. 331.

religious man rested on the words: "His hands were made strong by the mighty God of Israel"?

In his farewell address delivered on September 17, 1796, Washington said: "Of all the dispositions and habits which lead to political prosperity, religion and morality are indispensable supports. In vain would that man claim the tribute of patriotism who should labor to subvert these great pillars of human happiness—these firmest props of the duties of men and citizens. The mere politician, equally with the pious man, ought to respect and to cherish them. A volume could not trace all their connections with private and public felicity. Let it simply be asked, Where is the security for property, for reputation, for life, if the sense of religious obligation desert the oaths which are the instruments of investigation in courts of justice? And let us with caution indulge the supposition that morality can be maintained without religion. Whatever may be conceded to the influence of refined education on minds of peculiar structure, reason, and experience both forbid us to expect that national morality can prevail in exclusion of religious principle."

The versatility of Benjamin Franklin makes it difficult to label a man who excelled in so many fields; statesman, diplomatist, author, inventor and philosopher, his resources were endless.

He was one of the signers of the Declaration of Independence and in 1776 Congress sent him as a commissioner to Paris where he wrote constantly for the press and, "Kept the world constantly talking of him, and wondering at the inexhaustible variety, and unconventional novelty of his resources." A eulogy, often quoted, still bears repetition: "Such a servant, citizen, and patriot no other country ever had in the history of man."

"To suppose that Franklin was anti-religious or even indifferent would, in any case, be an egregious error. He contributed regularly to the church and responded to many appeals for gifts to various religious enterprises. He attended public worship with considerable frequency, declining to do so when he found the sermons too dogmatic, obscurantist or dull. As to his reason for quitting the preaching of one church he has left us a record, which sheds no little light on his religious attitudes. The minister took as his point of departure Paul's great saying, 'Whatsoever things are true, honest, just, pure, lovely or of good report; if there be any virtue and if there be any praise, think on these things.' 'And I imagined,' comments Franklin, 'in a sermon on such a text, we could not miss of having some morality.' But the discourse emphasized only the 'morality' of keeping the Sabbath day, reading the Scriptures, going to church, partaking of the sacrament, and paying due respect to the ministry!" [10]

On one occasion, when the question of opening the Constitutional Convention with prayer was being considered, he said: "The longer I live, the more convincing proofs I see of this truth, *that God governs in the affairs of men*. And if a sparrow cannot fall to the ground without His notice, is

---

[10] *The Amazing Benjamin Franklin*, pp. 94 and 95.

it probable that an empire can rise without His aid? We have been assured, Sir, in the Sacred Writings, that 'except the Lord build the house, they labour in vain that build it!' I firmly believe this; and I also believe, that, without His concurring aid, we shall succeed in this political building no better than the builders of Babel."

Naturally he was little interested in religious dogma and when his parents wrote to Benjamin expressing grief over some of his son's views, he replied: "My mother grieves that one of her sons is an Arian, another an Arminian. What an Arminian or an Arian is, I cannot say that I very well know. The truth is, I make such distinctions very little my study. I think vital religion has always suffered when orthodoxy is more regarded than virtue; and the Scriptures assure me, that at the last day we shall not be examined for what we *thought,* but what we *did;* and our recommendation will not be, that we said, Lord! Lord! but that we did good to our fellow creatures. See Matthew XXV."

There are some utterances of Franklin that are frankly sceptical and reveal much indecision on religious matters. In a recent and thoroughly discriminating biography of him by Bernard Fay, he points out that in America, Franklin was considered a Christian while in France he was classed with the atheists. Concerning his closing months, however, the same author says: "When he spoke of God he was as vague as he was tender, and far from reproaching Him for the evils he had received, he thanked Him for having sent so few. As the days passed he seemed more and more inclined

to take up the subject." [11]   Again, when he felt the approach
of death he said: "These pains will soon be over. They are
for my good; and, besides, what are the pains of a moment
in comparison with the pleasures of eternity?"

It is almost impossible to read any speech of Abraham
Lincoln without seeing the influence of the Bible upon his
life. There are very few speeches delivered during the last
seven years of his life, which do not contain direct quotations
from Scripture. Speaking of Lincoln's amazing knowledge
and apt use of the Bible, Bishop Simpson said in his address
at Lincoln's funeral: "He read his Bible frequently; he
loved it for its great truths; and he tried to be guided by its
precepts. He believed in Christ as the Saviour of sinners
and I think he was sincere in trying to bring his life into
harmony with the precepts of revealed religion. I doubt
if any President has shown such trust in God, or in public
document so frequently referred to divine aid."

In an address delivered before the American Bible Society
in 1901, Theodore Roosevelt said: "Lincoln built up his
entire reading upon his study of the Bible. He had mastered
it absolutely, mastered it as later he mastered only one or two
other books, mastered it until he became almost a man of one
book. He knew the Bible and put into practice what he had
been taught therein, and he left his life as part of the crown-
ing work of the century just closed." [12]

On January 12, 1851, Lincoln wrote to his stepbrother,

---

[11] Bernard Fay, *Franklin, the Apostle of Modern Times*, p. 509.
[12] S. Trevena Jackson, *Lincoln's Use of the Bible*, p. 10.

John D. Johnston, concerning his father who was very ill, saying: "I sincerely hope father may recover his health, but, at all events, tell him to remember to call upon and confide in our great and good and merciful Maker, who will not turn away from him in any extremity. He notes the fall of a sparrow, and numbers the hairs of our heads, and He will not forget the dying man who puts his trust in Him. Say to him that if we could meet now it is doubtful whether it would not be more painful than pleasant, but that if it be his lot to go now, he will soon have a joyous meeting with many loved ones gone before, and where the rest of us, through the help of God, hope ere long to join them." [13]

On September 7, 1864, a committee of coloured people in the city of Baltimore presented Lincoln with a Bible and, in acknowledging the gift, he said: "In regard to this great gift I have but to say: It is the best gift God has given to man. All the good Saviour gave to the world is communicated through this book. But for it we could not know right from wrong. All things most desirable for man's welfare, here and hereafter, are to be found portrayed in it. To you I return my most sincere thanks for the very elegant copy of the great Book of God which you present." Who could read this passage, from a conversation he had with Bateman, without realizing how deep were Lincoln's religious convictions? He said: "I know there is a God and that He hates injustice and slavery. I see the storm coming and I know that His hand is in it. If He has a place for me—and I

---

[13] William J. Johnstone, *Abraham Lincoln the Christian*, p. 58.

think He has—I believe I am ready. I am nothing, but truth is everything. I know I am right for Christ teaches it, and Christ is God."

A political contemporary of Daniel Webster referred to him as "The greatest orator that has ever lived in the Western Hemisphere." Whatever opinions men may have regarding Webster's political views or of some of the decisions he made, there is no question as to his intense patriotism and his extraordinary personal magnetism. His career, which closed on October 24, 1852, is one of the most colourful in an age of picturesque personalities.

Webster's father was an uncompromising Puritan and while Daniel in matters of conduct often differed from his father and his brother, there is reason to believe that his views were much the same as theirs. Disappointment clouded the closing months of Webster's career, but his reverence and sense of responsibility to God—always strong—deepened as the end drew near.

"As time passed Webster felt more and more keenly the injustice done him. Bitterness poisoned his days, and sorrow shortened his life. When the autumn came, he made ready for the end, knowing he would not survive another winter. One October morning Webster said to his physician, 'I shall die tonight.' The physician, an old friend, answered, 'You are right, sir.' When the twilight fell, and all had gathered about his bedside, Mr. Webster, in a tone that could be heard throughout the house, slowly uttered these words, 'My general wish on earth has been to do my Master's will. That there is a God, all must acknowledge. I see Him in all these wondrous works, Himself how wondrous! What would be the condition of any of us if we had not the hope of immortality? What ground is there to rest upon but the gospel? There were scattered hopes of the immortality of the soul, especially amongst the Jews. The Jews believed in a spiritual origin of creation; the Romans never reached it; the Greeks never reached it. It is a tradition that communication was made to the Jews by God Himself through Moses. There were intimations crepuscular, but—but—but —thank God! the gospel of Jesus Christ brought immortality to light, rescued it, brought it to light.' " [14]

Theodore Roosevelt might with almost equal appropriateness have been included amongst the great soldiers as in this chapter but it is reasonably certain that future generations will recall his statesmanlike qualities rather than his part in military affairs.

In answer to a letter of enquiry concerning his religious beliefs, the late Ex-president, Warren Harding, wrote on January 6, 1921: "Replying to your letter December 21 in which you request some expression from me concerning my impressions of 'Theodore Roosevelt the Christian'—Permit me to say that I am convinced that Theodore Roosevelt had a devout belief in God and though a consistent churchman he never paraded his belief, but it was evident in his writings, in his speeches and in his conduct. His clean personal life is the best proof of his faith and belief.

[14] Newell Dwight Hillis, *The Battle of Principles*, pp. 65 and 66.

"That he was a close student of the Bible was but natural since he was ever a seeker after Truth. Unquestionably he believed in prayer, not only as a means of grace, but as a personal help and consolation." [15]

"Religion was as natural to Mr. Roosevelt as breathing. It blended with his whole life as colour does with the rose. He did not need to constantly proclaim its presence any more than he did his sturdy health. And yet he recognized that it made requirements as certain as did his alert brain. He exhibited the presence of religion in his life in deed and declaration as he did his thought in spoken and written word. But he also just as certainly gave religion credit for early inspiration and direction as he did Harvard for helping him prepare for his lifework. When necessary and opportune Mr. Roosevelt would as naturally announce himself to be a Christian as he would that he was a loyal American. He was not satisfied merely to give evidence that he was an American by a consistent life, but he frequently and publicly proclaimed it. But even that was not sufficient; he further affirmed it by joining organizations known to stand for pure Americanism and then added a share of his talents to make those organizations successful in spreading American doctrines. Could he be less consistent with his religion? No, and therefore he announced himself a Christian by joining the church as the institution standing for the Christian religion and organized to spread it in all the world. He did not

[15] Letter to Rev. Christian F. Reisner.

wait for an opportune time, but facing it as a duty he acted." [16]

President Woodrow Wilson lived too recently for any true appraisal of his character to have been formulated. The fires of prejudice and political feeling have not fully died down.

His name will always be associated with the Great War and whatever views men may hold regarding his wisdom, few, if any, will question his absolute sincerity. "Mr. Wilson publicly proclaimed his spiritual guidance. It was not the first time that he had invoked the favor of the Almighty, and more than once it had been asked whether to Mr. Wilson religion was simply a conventionality or part of his life. Men who knew him best and had been given opportunities to form a judgement, said that Mr. Wilson was deeply religious. He was, said one observer, a Scotch Presbyterian, a Cromwellian, but with none of the austerity of the Covenanter; in him the fanaticism of his forbears had been softened and made gentle; he saw that existence was a perfectly ordered scheme. Less concerned about dogma or doctrine than the true spirit of Christianity, for between life and doctrine, Mr. Wilson said in one of his addresses, there was no real antithesis; a man 'lives upon a doctrine, upon a principle, upon an idea'; unconcerned about creeds and tolerant of formularies, the Supreme Being was not terrible and vengeful, always demanding retribution, but a loving Father, kind, forbearing, generous." [17]

---

[16] Christian F. Reisner, *Roosevelt's Religion*, p. 324.
[17] A. Maurice Low, *Woodrow Wilson, An Interpretation*, p. 184.

In an address delivered before a church assembly in Washington on April 8, 1915, Mr. Wilson uttered his conviction that men who fought for what was eternally right, must prevail. He said: "Then all about them, all about us, there sits the silent, waiting tribunal which is going to utter the ultimate judgement upon this struggle, the great tribunal of the opinion of the world; and I fancy that I see, I hope that I see, I pray that it may be that I do truly see, great spiritual forces lying waiting for the outcome of this thing to assert themselves, and asserting themselves even now, to enlighten our judgement and steady our spirits." We wish to see certain things triumph, the President said, but why do we wish to see them triumph, and what is there in them for the lasting benefit of mankind? "For we are not in this world to amuse ourselves with its affairs. We are here to push the whole sluggish mass forward in some particular direction, and unless you know the direction in which you want to go your force is of no avail.

"Do you love righteousness? is what each one of us ought to ask himself, and if you love righteousness, are you ready to translate righteousness into action and be ashamed and afraid before no man? It seems to me, therefore, that it is worth suggesting to you that you are not sitting here merely to transact the business and express the ideals of a great church, but you are here also as part of the assize of humanity, to remind yourselves of the things that are permanent and eternal which, if we do not translate into action, we have failed in the fundamental things of our lives."

The following letter, pasted on the front leaf of New

Testaments distributed to American soldiers and sailors as they left for Europe in July, 1917, was written and signed by President Wilson: "The Bible is the word of life. I beg that you will read it and find this out for yourselves—read, not merely snatches here and there, but long passages that will be the road to the heart of it. You will find it full of the things you have wondered about, and been troubled about, all your lives, as men have been always, and the more you read the more it will become plain to you what things are worth while and what are not, what things make men happy —loyalty, right dealing, speaking the truth, readiness to give everything for what they think their duty, and, most of all, the wish that they may have the real approval of the Christ— who gave everything for them. . . . When you have read the Bible you will know that it is the Word of God, because you will have found it the key to your own heart, your own happiness and your own duty."